SANDI PATTI

SANDI PATTI

The Voice of Gospel

by
DON CUSIC

A DOLPHIN BOOK
Doubleday
NEW YORK
1988

Library of Congress Cataloging-in-Publication Data

Cusic, Don.
Sandi Patti, the voice of gospel.

"A Dolphin book."
1. Patti, Sandi. 2. Singers—United States—Biography.
I. Title.
ML420.P322C9 1988 783.7'092'4 [B] 87-27444
ISBN 0-385-24353-7

Printed in the United States of America
First Edition

For more reasons than I can name,
this book is dedicated to Jackie.

Acknowledgments

The author would like to thank—for various reasons and to varying degrees—the following: Ron Patty, Cindy Morton, Marty McCall, Niles Borup, Paul Baker, Gary McSpadden, Don Boyer, Bill Gaither, John Styll, Walt Quinn, Don Butler, J. Aaron Brown, Kelly Delaney, Robert Oermann, Charles Wolfe, John and Bev Darnall, Bob Millard, Scott Pelking, Greg Nelson, Don Butler and the Gospel Music Association, the staffs at the Anderson Public Library and the Anderson College Library, the Todd Library at Middle Tennessee State University (especially Betty McFall), Crawford High School in San Diego, and, of course, Sandi Patti Helvering.

A very special thanks to the Center for Popular Music at Middle Tennessee State University in Murfreesboro, Tennessee (especially Paul Wells, Ellen Garrison, and Sarah Long), secretaries Sandra Neely, Shannon Jones, Deborah Robinson, and Janice Bursyek.

Extra special thanks to agent Madeleine Morel, editor Casey Fuetsch, A. Joseph Guffey for giving me encouragement as a writer, Charles Molitor for my first job with a newspaper, and Johnstone Campbell for showing how to appreciate writing and literature. Also to Delaney, Jesse, and Eli, just for being who they are.

Prologue

Sandi Helvering's eyes open quickly. The soft light of the clock shows 1:22 A.M. *The door to her bedroom is open and she can hear her baby crying. Quickly, she gets out of bed and enters her eight-month-old daughter's room and picks her up. "Oh, it's all right," she says. "Shhhh. Let's check your diaper."*

When Sandi has finished changing Anna and snapping the sleeping gown back into place, she sits in the rocking chair and begins feeding her baby. Sandi looks down on the tiny face and hands and an overwhelming feeling of love comes over her, like a blanket that covers them both. In the couple's bedroom, John Helvering is still asleep.

Sandi leans her head back against the rocking chair and thinks of her life. A week ago, she was singing in front of thousands of people, hearing thunderous applause. Many had wanted to meet her, to talk with her, touch her, get an autograph, say a word of encouragement, just say they had met her. She kept these moments brief because she wanted to be with her precious daughter. Her husband John was protective and polite and handled it all well—she spent a few moments with some people backstage, then was left alone with Anna.

It feels as if God is in the dimly lit bedroom, a warm spirit hovering over Sandi and her child. Just as Sandi holds Anna close, she feels herself being held close by the Heavenly Father. It is a good time for more reflection.

Sandi loves the stage, she loves singing, and she loves the applause. It is a comfortable feeling to be able to go into a strange town and have thousands of people come just to hear you sing. Sometimes it is scary that strangers know so much, but it is also reassuring. She is loved, she is appreciated. Who could ask for more?

But it's more than just being a star. Sandi feels that when God looks at her, He does so with a smile and a nod. "You are My child," He seems to say. "Go and sing. It is My will. It is My wish. I will bless you when you do this." Sometimes, when her husband John tells her about a series of concerts or a tour, a small voice says, "Oh no, not that again. But I want to stay here in Anderson in my home with Anna. I want to be 'normal.' " But even as she feels it, she knows it isn't really true. Yes, she loves her home and her family, but she also loves the stage and the concerts. The singing is like a magnet pulling her toward the spotlight. Though Sandi has said she never dreamed of being a big star, she knows that something deep inside her always wanted this.

Sandi followed her heart when she majored in music education in college. She did not know that one day there would be gold records on the wall or Grammy and Dove awards in a trophy case, but she knew she would be singing. An old Swedish proverb says: "Whoever sings will always find a song." Sandi found her song and she sings it. Along the way she discovered a secret to true happiness: Be who you are and do what you love.

It is almost two o'clock in the morning. Gently, she gets up from the rocking chair, still holding her daughter close. Sandi walks over to the crib and puts Anna down softly, never taking her eyes off the baby. John stirs slightly.

Sandi Patti must reconcile her two lives, but she will not accomplish this by thinking long and deep into the night. She will simply get up in the morning and do it. Now she must get some sleep. Sandi listens for her child's cry as her own eyes close. She snuggles on the pillow and drifts off to sleep.

SANDI PATTI

1

There are about eight thousand people in the civic arena and the only reason it is not a total sellout is because the promoter did not sell the seats behind the stage. Since Sandi Patti does not perform in the round, those seats would give a horrible view and it is not worth making customers unhappy. The crowd is an interesting mixture of young and old, with parents, grandparents, and kids all over the place. These are all good, solid, middle-class Americans, clean-cut and well-behaved. The young people, while dressed a bit modish, are definitely not part of the punk movement.

At the back of the stage is a blue curtain with SANDI PATTI written across it in her script logo. To the left is a baby grand piano as well as a cluster of synthesizers and computers. On the left side of the stage are three microphones and three tall chairs. There are potted plants scattered about.

Dick Tunney has come out first and sits down at the keyboards. He is young and handsome and dressed in a white suit with an open collar. There are pink and purple lights flashing—Sandi's favorite colors—and the electronic music begins swirling. Then First Call comes out. Comprised of Marty McCall, Bonnie Keen, and Melody Tunney (Dick's wife), the group is smiling and walking briskly to the three microphones. They are dressed in black. Then Sandi, dressed in a bright red dress, comes out from behind the stage. She walks through the smoke and goes directly to the center microphone, where she begins to sing "Let There Be Praise."

During the song, Sandi's finger points up and some members of the audience do the same; then she raises her hands and throws herself into the song. After she is finished, there is much clapping and she says, "We are here tonight for one reason: to worship Jesus Christ as Lord!"

Sandi knows her audience well because she and they are one. These are people from the Christian culture who go to church on Sunday and Wednesday nights. Many sing in a choir on Sundays at their church.

Sandi shouts out, "We've come to celebrate the King!" as Dick plays a piano intro. Then Sandi launches into "Upon This Rock." At the end of the song, after the applause, Sandi thanks the crowd for being so wonderful. Then she encourages them to feel free to worship, say "Amen," sing along, smile, or raise their hands before she gently admonishes them: "If you've got to frown, *go home!*" The crowd laughs and applauds.

Sandi then sings "Love in Any Language," which begins with "I love you" in several different languages. The song was written by Jon Mohr and John Mays and strikes a deep chord in Sandi's international audiences (it was a big hit when she performed it in De Bron, Holland, at the Christian Artists Seminar there). As Sandi sings, she paces before the audience, brimming with forceful self-confidence while a young fan comes up and puts some roses on the edge of the stage.

Next First Call sings their song "Undivided." Marty McCall begins with his powerful voice before the two women in the group, Bonnie Keen and Melody Tunney, join in, blending together harmoniously. The song, written by Melody Tunney, makes a strong statement for Christian unity, which is compatible with Sandi's message. Melody and her husband Dick have written a number of songs for Sandi.

First Call, with their charismatic stage presence and tight harmonies, adds some pizzazz to the show. Sandi does not perform with a band—only taped accompaniment tracks—so she needs some help when she presents a two-and-a-half-hour show. Opting to not have an opening act, she includes First Call in her show as background singers while letting them do some numbers of their own. This is just the way she got her start with the Bill Gaither Trio. And it was when she had her moment in the spotlight and sang "We Shall Behold Him" that audiences discovered Sandi Patti. That song launched her career. She's learned a lot of lessons from Bill Gaither and now her own show is an updated version of his performances. The supreme irony is that she has, in a sense, copied many of Gaither's tactics and replaced him as the major act in the church world, reaching heights he could never reach because he came along as a trailblazer and had to lay the groundwork for so much of contemporary Christian music. And now Sandi is reaping the rewards of Gaither's pioneering efforts while Gaither is moving into the ranks of "legend" status.

Walking over to the piano and introducing Dick Tunney, Sandi strikes up a mock conversation about kids, prompting Dick to pull out a wallet full of pictures of his own child in a mildly comic routine before bringing Sandi's daughter out onstage.

Little Anna ("Ahn-na") goes to the front of the stage with Courtney Keen, daughter of Dan and Bonnie, and the petite duo sings a little song while Sandi stands and watches with parental pride.

After a performance of "Shine Down," Sandi talks about the Friendship Club, which is an organization she and the Helvering Agency have created for kids. She invites kids to send in their names and addresses—there are currently thirty thousand in the club—so they can get free coloring books and information on Sandi. It is a successful marketing tool, one that McDonald's also uses, because it ensures a growing market. No wonder the kids all love her.

She invites all kids eight and under to come up on the stage and they do so in droves. After she gets this crowd up onstage, she rehearses them to sway back and forth in time to the music, to bow their heads at the right time, and then to "snap to" like soldiers. Finally she begins the song "Purest Praise" as the kids move to the music. This section must remind Sandi of her days in San Diego when she was working with the children's choir at the church where her father was minister of music.

O.K., you guys, today we're going to learn a new song—Paul, are you listening?—and here is the music. Christy, I need for you to stop talking when I'm talking, O.K.? It's called "There Is a Fountain" and it has a real pretty melody. All together now.

You guys are really doing a good job! Now remember—Michael and Zachary, do you want to be in this choir or not? What is it, Jennifer? Yes, you can be excused. And I want you to hold that last phrase. Be sure to enunciate! *That means say all your words* clearly! *Now, let's try it one more time.*

The crowd loves it.

2

The Crucifixion of Jesus lends itself to theater perhaps better than any other story. Here you have the pure individual, standing alone against the world, misunderstood to the point that His holy mission is the cause for His death. The death of an "innocent" is always powerful drama and, in the Christian story, Jesus is the *most* innocent person who ever lived. The songs "A Morning Like This" and "Via Dolorosa" are good examples: The ageless story of Christ's death and Resurrection are told again.

An essential appeal of an artist like Sandi Patti is that she embodies this sense of drama so well. Only someone raised within the church, amid all the restrictions and taboos and warnings about secular drama, can intrinsically sense this need for drama by the church audience. Strong emotions are allowed to surface in a controlled, sanctified environment and the age-old problem of retelling this well-known story is solved by this sense of urgency, a new twist, a dramatic performance that pulls out the emotions and lifts the soul to a new level. When the climax comes, a new insight is discovered when Sandi talks about a "deeper walk with the Lord"—it is one which opens the curtains in the theater of the heart and soul. It is powerful stuff and the performer draws the emotions from the audience.

Anyone who stands before an audience is engaged in "performance" and they are expected to "move" that audience, which is the essence of theater. The Christian culture has adopted their own vocabularly—or Christianese—for this. They insist on the word "bless" instead of "move" (i.e., "I was really *blessed* by that concert") and "communication" instead of "performance" (i.e., "She really *communicates* with an audience"), while "theater" or "drama" is replaced by "service" or "concert." Still, though the theatrical terms are cast aside, a strong element of theater and drama encases the whole event. This is done with individual songs as well as with the concert as a whole.

A dramatic highlight of Sandi's shows occurs when she performs "Via Dolorosa." The Via Dolorosa (or "Way of Sorrows") is the street in Jerusalem where Jesus carried His cross on the way to His Crucifixion on Calvary Hill. In her video of this song, Sandi walks down the Via Dolorosa and stops, striking some melodramatic poses, suitably pensive to indicate deep thought about Jesus and all that the Crucifixion means. Along the way she picks up a rose, which she discards later in the video in an attempt to symbolize the ending of His life. In her concerts, Sandi often tells of walking down the Via Dolorosa and then seeing the tomb "where He is no longer."

"Via Dolorosa" was written by Niles Borup and Billy Sprague and won the Dove Award for Song of the Year in 1986. According to Borup, he got the idea for the song while watching the evening news on a Good Friday in 1982 or 1983. On the news was the Pope doing the stations of the cross on the Via Dolorosa, where Jesus walked. As the newscaster gave his report, Niles grabbed a pencil. "I was hoping they would say that title again—and they did," he said. "I wrote it down and then looked it up in my Latin dictionary because I didn't know what it meant."

Borup notes that there were some other songs with Hebrew in them about this time—"El Shaddai" being the most popular—and when he presented this idea of "Via Dolorosa" to other writers he was writing songs with, they all turned it down because they thought the concept had been "overdone." Finally Niles and Billy

Sprague were together one day to write songs and Niles told his idea to Billy "and he almost fell out of his chair," reports Niles.

"We wrote it in about two hours," said Niles. "It just seemed to flow. Billy was playing the guitar and had a major part in the melody—he came up with the Spanish feel." After completing the song, each writer played it for his individual publisher and the publishers each got excited and called Greg Nelson, Sandi's producer. He loved it and immediately put it on "hold," which meant the writers and publishers agreed not to play the song for anyone else. It would remain on "hold" for two years before Sandi recorded it.

Just before she recorded the song, there was another little drama which almost caused the song to never see the light of day. According to Niles, "There was another song called 'Via Dolorosa' by Dennis Agajanian and there was an advertisement for that song on the front cover of *MusicLine* [a gospel trade magazine]. Some of those involved in Sandi's album called the publishers and told them, 'If the Agajanian song gets on the charts, we're not cutting your "Via Dolorosa." ' " Fortunately for Billy and Niles—and then for Sandi—the other "Via Dolorosa" never made the charts.

Sandi goes from "Via Dolorosa" in her concert to an old hymn, "The Old Rugged Cross," as the Crucifixion story moves along, and then to "Was It a Morning Like This," which is about the Resurrection of Christ.

This is highly emotional for the audience as well as Sandi, and the air is charged as the Greatest Story Ever Told is retold again. It is the essence of Christianity—this ignominious death and glorious Resurrection by Jesus—and it affirms the most basic belief of this audience: Jesus was more than a man, He was the *Son of God!*

When this medley of songs is finished, the smoke is pouring forth from the back of the stage again and the blue lights are on. It has become obvious during the concert that on each song the lights start relatively low and, as the song progresses and swells, the lights get brighter. It is highlighted by the singer in a dramatic pose and Sandi plays her part well, standing with her arms outstretched as if she is on the cross, her head hung to one side, imitating the dying Jesus as the lights go out except for some back lighting, which shows her silhouette to the audience just before intermission.

With this, Sandi and the singers exit the stage.

3

Indiana State Route 32 is a major four-lane highway that goes through Anderson, Indiana. Travelers on Route 32 will go past some Delco-Remy plants that have been a major economic backbone for Anderson since the 1930s, past the Mounds Mall on the left, and right on to Muncie, about ten miles up the road from Anderson. If you take Route 9 instead, you will head straight north to Alexandria, which is headquarters for Bill Gaither's organization and the home of Pinebrook Studio and the Barn recording studio, where Sandi sang some of her first commercials and where she still goes to record some of her latest records.

The city proper of Anderson lies to the left of Route 32. Flat Indiana farmland with its rich black dirt surrounds the city. In the winter, cornstalks stick up through the snow; in the spring, it is lush and green with the crops of corn, wheat, and soybeans coming up and covering the area like huge blankets. But the farmland is disappearing as the family farms go under and around Anderson new buildings and housing developments stand where crops used to be.

The area was first settled in 1823 by John Berry. It was the sight of a Delaware Indian tribe village at the time, ruled by Chief Kikthawanund (Kik-tha-we-nund). When he introduced himself to Berry, the white man smiled and said, "Nice to meet you, Captain Anderson." Then Mr. Berry named the place Andersontown.

Indiana became the nineteenth state in 1816, sixteen years after Congress had established the Indiana Territory. The early history of the state is filled with stories of Indian battles, including the famous battle of Tippecanoe in 1811 when General William Henry Harrison defeated Tecumseh's Indian confederation. The term "Hoosiers" probably came from the early habit of people calling out "Who's there?" when visitors came, although it may also be the derivative of "husher," a slang term given to a fighting man who could "hush" others with his fists.

In 1886 natural gas was discovered in the area and the region became important as a boom followed. This gas pocket was worked until the end of the century, when it ran out and the boomers left town.

The next big thing to happen to Anderson occurred in 1927 when General Motors established its Delco-Remy division there. The 550-acre, sixteen-plant operation has been the county's largest employer since it first opened its doors, accounting for 30 percent of the employment at one time and providing 16,200 jobs. However, as America shifted from an industrial nation to an information-based economy in the 1970s—and the gas shortages in the late 1970s made American gas guzzlers less desirable than the smaller Japanese-made automobiles—the fortunes of General Motors and Anderson have been declining. Too, as companies did expand, they went South, where the labor was cheaper, the unions weaker, and the air warmer. General Motors did that when it expanded by opening plants in Mississippi and Georgia in the mid-1970s. The end result is that Anderson has been hit hard by the industrial decline, even more pronounced in the 1980s, and people have been fleeing the city rather than flocking to it.

John and Sandi Patti Helvering live in a small subdivision east of Anderson. Their home is a large two-story green house with a two-car garage attached. Out back, inside the tall wooden fence, is a swimming pool, while inside the big roomy house is a fireplace and comfortable furnishings. The house was purchased by John and Sandi in 1982 and is only the second place they have lived since they were married. It is located on a small quiet street that leads to a dead end. It could be Ozzie and Harriet's neighborhood, or Wally and the Beaver's home—nice and comfortable although not ostentatious.

To the west is Anderson College, the heart and home of Sandi Patti country; nearby is the Park Place Church of God, a large church with a playground in its courtyard, offices and classrooms, and a chapel that has a large stained-glass window on the curved back wall. On the side walls are tall windows of plain glass and the brown wooden pews sit on each side of the long narrow aisle that leads to the altar and the pulpit, which protrudes just to the left of the altar. The inside of the church is shaped like a cross. This is where Sandi Patti worships—her spiritual home—and the church where she did much of her performing when she was in college.

There have been three geographical pockets where contemporary Christian music has flowered in America and Anderson is one of them. The first was Southern California—particularly Orange County—where the Calvary Chapel, headed by pastor Chuck Smith, was a haven for those involved in the early Jesus Movement. Among the artists who came from this area are 2nd Chapter of Acts, Keith Green, Love Song, Chuck Girrard, Karen Lafferty, and the whole Maranatha! Music movement, which released one of the first Jesus rock albums, as well as a series of "praise albums" that have created that genre of soft worship music as a major arm of contemporary Christian music.

The next area to develop was Nashville, particularly the Belmont Church headed by pastor Don Finto. Located on Music Row, the church sits across a side street from Koinonia, a Christian coffeehouse where artists such as Amy Grant, Gary Chapman, Brown Bannister, Kathy Trocolli, Dogwood, Steve and Annie Chapman, Chris Christian, and others honed their performing skills. (It may be argued that Abilene Christian University in Texas is another pocket, but those from that school gravitated to Nashville, where they made their influence felt.)

The third wellspring for gospel music is Anderson College. It has become a center for music because of the rich legacy provided by the Church of God, headquartered in Anderson. This church was never afraid of singing and, indeed, promoted much of its doctrines through songs in books like *Reformation Glory* and others published by the Church of God organization (formerly the Gospel Trumpet Company). This reformation church sent out a number of evangelists in the early part of this century, and accompanying these evangelists were singers who sang in railroad stations, homes, schoolhouses, or street corners, and anywhere else they thought they might attract a crowd.

Each of these areas has reached a slightly different audience with its music (although, of course, there is much overlapping). The California movement was originally street-level rock music aimed at kids outside the church. The music from Nashville has generally been aimed at the Christian consumer who goes to church but wants some good music on the radio and *outside* the church. This music is directed toward the people who want to get outside the church but not away from Christianity—a music geared toward radio and records/tapes for the home and car. Anderson, on the other hand, is the great source of music *for* the church. Singers such as Sandi Patti, Steve Green, and the Gaithers—artists whose music fits best in the church—are echoed here by church choirs and their voices (especially Sandi's and Steve's) are essentially that of the quintessential church soloist.

The person most responsible for making Anderson a center for this type of music is Bill Gaither. Beginning in the mid-1960s with his group, the Bill Gaither Trio, Gaither and his wife Gloria have written songs aimed directly at the church audience. Gaither and his group emerged as the major selling gospel group in the 1960s, having the first gold album on a Christian label (Benson) with an album by Christian artists—*Alleluia, a Praise Gathering for Believers*—in 1977. Bill himself has emerged as the godfather of contemporary Christian music from his songwriting talent, his success as an artist in concerts and on record, and his business acumen, which led him to establish a major organization that includes publishing, booking, printing, and recording.

Gaither, a graduate of Anderson College, did not leave his native area to set up his headquarters. Because he put his base of operations in Alexandria—just ten miles up the road from the college—and kept his home in the area, he provided an outlet for other local talent to grow. A major reason for the success of Sandi Patti is because of the opportunities provided by Bill Gaither through his Pinebrook Studio (where she sang commercials), his tours (where she sang backup and performed solo numbers), and his booking agency (which booked her tours until 1987 and provided her with a performing platform). In fact, the Helvering Agency and the whole organization now surrounding Sandi (including the new office complex being built) is modeled on Gaither's operation.

For a number of years Sandi's organization, the Helvering Agency, run by husband John, was located at 530 Grand Avenue, just a few blocks from the Anderson campus in a white frame house perched atop a small hill. John and Sandi lived there and it evolved into an office until they simply outgrew it. Their new office is located at the north of town. Here, on a large plot of land with a large pond, they have built an office complex called 2200 Madison Square that provides plenty of room for their whole operation.

It is hard to describe Anderson without invoking the memory of Norman Rockwell because the town looks as if it could easily be the setting for his paintings. A Republican town—and elections generally always go in that direction in this area known as the "Republican heartland"—it has managed to retain a small town feel about it, although it could more accurately be described as a small city. It is what America used to be and maybe, at her heart, still is. It is a town of good people, straightforward and conservative, who are both friendly to strangers and wary of them. Just like most other towns, it has rich and poor folks. But it is primarily the home of the type of middle-class people who are the backbone of this country, who go to work every morning and come home every evening and want an honest day's pay for an honest day's work. But the town has also tasted greed from the high wages paid by General Motors and now is a bit afraid of the future without Delco-Remy—which gave the town jobs as well as an identity—because people are moving out and a new age is moving in that doesn't have large factories and big smokestacks as its trademarks.

You've got to know Anderson—or at least some town like it—to understand John Helvering and Sandi Patti. They are still small town people, although they move in a big-time orbit now. But their values, their thinking, their way of looking at things is linked closely with a small town. And it is linked even closer with the atmosphere of a small Christian college in a small town. This college is part of their family and Anderson is the home to which they always return no matter how far their travels have taken them.

4

The Church of God Reformed began when Daniel S. Warner declared in 1881 in Beaver Dam, Indiana, that he was forever free from sects and embraced twice-born believers everywhere. This young upstart was known as a troublemaker by his denomination, who had expelled him for holiness preaching in a Findlay, Ohio, meeting. Warner attended Ohio's Oberlin College and had been exposed to evangelist-president Charles Grandison Finney, who was one of the country's most famous preachers around the time of the Civil War.

Warner was first and foremost an evangelist—his mission was to proclaim the Good News and lead people out of sin and into holiness. He married Tamzen Ann Kerr in 1867, but his wife died after giving birth to triplet daughters, who also all died.

After his conversion, Warner joined the ministry with the Churches of God of North America, sometimes referred to as the Winebrennarians because they had been formed by John Winebrenner, a German Reformed minister who had been influenced heavily by the revivalism of the early 1800s. The West Ohio Eldership of the Churches of God licensed him to preach in 1872 and in 1874 he married again at age thirty-one, this time to Sarah Keller, an eighteen-year-old woman, and they moved to Seward, Nebraska, where, amid the vast, open prairies, he set out to do home missionary work. In 1875 they returned to Ohio, where a baby girl was born. After the death of the girl at age three, Warner's wife abandoned him and their young son Sidney and went to live in Cincinnati. He did not remarry until after her death, a number of years later.

After Warner's license to preach was revoked in January 1878 and he was expelled from the Eldership, he spent the next seventeen years of his life launching and extending the Church of God Reformation movement across the country. He believed in a radical Christianity with obedience to the call of God being total and unconditional. He scathingly denounced sects to people, who responded by "coming out" (leaving their denomination). When he called for holiness, people came to the altar to be "sanctified." He preached intensely against organization of any kind within the church because he believed the body of true believers was the only true church and could never be organized by man. Warner also felt that holiness—living a clean, spotless, pure life—was the basis for Christian unity and he demanded this of believers.

In 1879 Warner purchased a half-interest in a holiness paper, *The Herald of Gospel Freedom,* for $250. This paper was owned by I. W. Lowman and sponsored by the Eldership of Northern Indiana. The next year Warner's name appeared alone as editor and the paper was merged with a holiness paper from Indianapolis called *The Pilgrim* to form a new paper called *The Trumpet.*

Although it moved six times in six years, always on the verge of bankruptcy, *The Trumpet* was a great unifying force for the "saints," which is the name given to the body of believers by the believers themselves.

Daniel Warner died in 1895 and the baton was passed to E. E. Byrum, who had attended several colleges and whose father had given him an inheritance, so, when his heart followed the reformation call, he provided some much-needed capital for the movement at an opportune time.

Byrum had met Warner when *The Trumpet* was owned by three people: Warner, a silent partner named Brother Michels, and J. C. Fisher, who had a mistress and was preparing to divorce his wife.

Warner did not want to associate with Fisher, but Fisher asked Warner for $1,000 for his share in *The Trumpet,* an impossible figure until Byrum arrived on the scene. Byrum's inheritance bought *The Trumpet,* which explains how, at Warner's death, Byrum and his brother Noah came to own the Trumpet Company.

Byrum ran the organization with an iron fist—he was publisher, business manager, managing editor, and overseer of every facet of the office. In 1895 (the year of Warner's death) there were seventy-five hundred copies of *The Trumpet* mailed out each month and three thousand regular subscribers. That same year the total number of tracts, songbooks, and other literature and material published by the company reached two million pieces. E. E. Byrum, sitting astride this organization, managed to keep a tight rein on the company for the next thirty years.

The Trumpet Company eventually moved to Anderson, Indiana, in 1908 because, with the gas boom ending, good land was cheap, there was access to rail transportation, and it had a good central location for the developing church population. The organization lived commune-style with no salaries paid and income dependent upon freewill offerings and the sale of books and tracts. In Anderson the first offices were a large U-shaped building constructed from timbers left from the St. Louis World's Fair. It later became the Main Building for Anderson College when that institution was formed and remained standing until it was replaced in 1970 by Decker Hall.

Schisms in the church occurred in the early years—one of the most serious from 1908 to 1914 over the issue of whether men could wear neckties. Usually it was the women who were heavily censored with their dress—no wedding bands, long, uncut hair braided and fixed on top of the head, no makeup, and no ornamentation of pins or jewelry of any kind were the rules. The true sanctified woman dressed plainly and showed no outward manifestations of resident carnality or conformity with "the world."

Regarding courtship, *The Trumpet* published an article in 1906 which stated that "genuine courtship is for those who are intending matrimony . . . [they should] sit at a reasonable distance from each other, look each other squarely in the face, and talk business. Above all, shun a giddy, funny, proud, fashion-loving woman, for she will make you ashamed, run you into debt, and let your house and children go to ruin. All kissing, fondling, and caressing should be left out of courtship, at least until after engagement, then indulged in very sparingly." About children, *The Trumpet* espoused that these young ones should "avoid such games that create evil, feed a spirit of ambition, and such indeed as do not stop with boys and girls but are played in gambling circles or houses of ill-fame. The larger children do not need much play. Under proper training, children, also young people, may be very profitably entertained at home by musical exercises and by teaching, walking exercises for recreation, and by Sunday school and Bible reading."

Divine healing was a central tenet in this early church and was viewed as giving authenticity and authority to the reformation movement. Byrum regarded healing as "part of our spiritual birthright" and stated that it comes "when the conditions are right. That is, one must clear away any sinful impediments of attitude, renounce any reliance on man-made remedies, call for the laying on of hands and anointment with oil, accept the promises of God and claim victory." For those who were not healed, there was a terminal guilt because the lack of healing implied some secret sin, lack of proper faith, or ungodliness.

Although founder Warner had toyed with the idea of beginning an educational arm of the Trumpet Company, E. E. Byrum was dead set against the notion. But when he stepped down in 1916, F. G. Smith was installed as editor of *The Trumpet* (the most powerful position in the church at the time) and J. T. Wilson initiated an educational venture as part of the company. Until this time, the only credentials for the ministry were "to be filled with the Holy Spirit and have a reasonable knowledge of the English language."

Frederick George Smith was one of the bright young lights of this movement when he assumed the editorship at the age of thirty-five. He had already published *What the Bible Teaches,* which became the most important book for this young church, giving the movement a "theological spine" and a "standard of orthodoxy" as he expounded on what the group should believe. Smith, like Warner, did not trust organization and often warned followers about the dangers of organizing a church. For him a believer "came under" or "got in line and stayed in line" and the "charismatic" process—endowment of gifts—was a function of the Holy Spirit alone, who divinely appointed the leaders of the church. Smith felt he was ordained by God to lead the company and that his writings held insights given by the Holy Spirit and were directed by God. For him the idea of a college was a great threat.

The Bible Training School began in 1917 and was held in the Trumpet workers' home. Young workers at the company, attending classes at night, were the first students. It was viewed with much skepticism by many of the leaders, who saw it as a diversionary burden, and it almost did not make it to its second year. Finally the Bible Training School was allowed to go on but was not allowed to give diplomas because these showed evidence of "worldly conformity."

The school—which was a two-year program at first—struggled along those first few years, surviving against a number of adversaries until 1925, when a charter was granted and the prohibition against degrees was lifted. That was the year George Russell Olt joined the faculty and began to build an accredited college and seminary for the church.

F. G. Smith had always wanted to eliminate or control the school. When the editorship of *The Trumpet* changed in 1930, some of the leaders still felt a threat from the school, which dealt in the marketplace of ideas, calling it a "mortal enemy standing in the way of divine fulfillment of the last reformation dream" and an institution which would "send out pastors with educational credentials in place of Holy Ghost ordination."

A major push to get rid of the school occurred in 1933, masterminded by F. G. Smith. Called "The Springfield Resolution," the main points against the school included the assertions that textbooks were introduced to students with "theories that contradicted standard Bible doctrine," and that "non-theological courses were causing much friction in the ministry." Another invective against the school, "The Toledo Resolution," was issued in the spring of 1934.

John Morrison, president of the school, fought back by unifying the home front, organizing the alumni (who had attained positions of leadership and key pastorates in the church), and, in a highly charged emotional vote held during camp meeting time in June 1934, marshaled just enough votes to keep the school. Since that time, Anderson College has remained on firm footing, providing an educational arm for the church, sending out leaders. It has established a central focal point for the movement, which eventually embraced, rather than disparaged, liberal arts education and learning.

Today Anderson College is a pretty campus with twenty-three buildings—mostly brick, with a touch of modernism in the architecture—on seventy-seven acres. It is a liberal arts college that requires chapel attendance and a solid dose of Bible and religious studies courses. It is assumed that all the students are Christians—the lady in the admissions office advises that the two letters of recommendation that accompany the application come from "a teacher and your minister"—and the headquarters for the Church of God (not to be confused with the one headquartered in Cleveland, Tennessee) is located right across from the campus.

The church and college have kept the tradition of "homecoming" and "camp meeting" alive and each year the week of college commencement witnesses about twenty thousand people connected with the Church of God coming to town for their annual get-together. There are a number of meetings, revivals, and church-related activities that begin with the commencement. For those involved with the Church of God Reformed, this is the highlight of the year, the one gathering they can't miss in order to stay in touch with old friends as well as the church itself.

Sandi Patti's picture is on the brochure with the application that Anderson College sends out to prospective students. Below the picture she writes that Anderson College has been "a very important part of my life" and that "the people on campus helped me identify both my spiritual and career goals." She continues that the people at Anderson "encouraged me to excel, and they helped me realize my musical ambitions." Sandi concludes: "Anderson College provided me with good memories, good friends, and a good education."

5

Floyd Tunnell entered Anderson College in 1937 to study for the ministry. Born in Canute, Oklahoma, on November 14, 1907, Tunnell was a dedicated minister and beside his picture in the 1941 yearbook is the inscription: THE LIFE OF A PIOUS MINISTER IS VISIBLE RHETORIC. Tunnell had married Mable Perry in Oklahoma and she also graduated from Anderson College. The couple had four children—Donald, Paul, Robert, and Carolyn—and after graduation, the Tunnells lived in various parts of the country as Floyd took pastorates in various Churches of God.

Carolyn Faye Tunnell, the second of the four children, was born on July 1, 1933, in Canute, Oklahoma. Carolyn had an early interest in music and began taking piano lessons when she was six. In 1951 Floyd Tunnell was living in Anderson, where he held the pastorate of the East Side Church of God, which had just opened its doors. Carolyn enrolled in Anderson College that fall as a piano major. (All four of the Tunnell children would follow in their parents' footsteps and graduate from Anderson: Robert in 1950, Carolyn in 1955, Donald in 1957, and Paul in 1965.)

Ronald Eugene Patty was born July 2, 1933—the day after Carolyn Tunnell—in Sapulpa, Oklahoma—about 150 miles away from his future wife. His father, Harry C. Patty (a factory worker) was born in Indiana; his mother, Grace Prye, was born in Missouri. He picked up the nickname "Tyke" when he was a youngster because his neighbors thought he was nothing but a "little tyke." By the time he arrived in Anderson, he was five feet ten inches tall and weighed 175 pounds, but the nickname still stuck.

Patty graduated from Sapulpa High School with honors in June 1951. He was a star athlete who lettered in three sports: football, basketball, and baseball. Patty also played trumpet in the school band all four years and sang in the choir. In his senior year he was chosen as an honorable mention for the Oklahoma state all-stars.

Entering college as a physical education major, Patty's plans at that time were to go into coaching. He defined his interests at that time as "anything churchified, sporty, or musical" and insisted he had no pet peeves or hobbies. A friendly outgoing youngster, filled with self-confidence and a gregariousness, Patty soon became popular at Anderson and often regaled his friends by singing and playing the trumpet.

When Ron Patty and Carolyn Tunnell entered Anderson College as freshmen in the fall of 1951, Harry Truman was President and the Korean War was raging. There had been a heat wave in Anderson in August that had temperatures hovering around 100 degrees each day and the city's water supply was drying up. Just after the college opened, on September 5, a peace treaty was signed in San Francisco, that aligned Japan, which was in the process of rebuilding, with the United States.

In the town of Anderson, a fifty-pound bag of potatoes was $1.29, apples were three pounds for $.20, men's suits ranged from $26.75 to $55.00, women's cotton dresses were $5.95. And an advertisement raved about a new "RCA Victor '45 Personal Phonograph" that played "up to 14 records" for $34.95.

The television era was in its infancy. There were black and white sets, but there was only one channel to watch in Anderson. Among the programs broadcast were "The Cisco Kid," "Mama," and "Man Against Crime." Local movie theaters showed *Bedtime for Bonzo, Little Egypt,* and Walt Disney's *Alice in Wonderland*, but students at Anderson were discouraged from going to the movies. Radio was still the main form of entertainment.

When classes began on September 12, 1951, there was excitement in the air, along with some anxiety—a number of young men were being drafted for the Korean War and some at Anderson would receive their notice. But out on the gridiron, the football team had a new star quarterback, Ron "Tyke" Patty, number 47. Although Anderson College finished dead last in its conference that season, Ron Patty ranked fourteenth among quarterbacks for small colleges in the nation. During that fall semester, a romance blossomed quickly for Ron Patty and Carolyn Tunnell.

The highlight of the next fall semester for Ron Patty occurred on Saturday, October 25, 1952, at the M. C. Formal. After the song "Let Me Call You Sweetheart" was sung, Eveleen Shriner announced that Ron Patty and Carolyn Tunnell were engaged. It was a big evening for Patty, who was president of the sophomore class as well as being a star athlete, and many of the girls on campus must have shed a few tears of disappointment at the announcement while Carolyn was bursting with joy.

On Monday, June 1, 1953, Ron Patty and Carolyn Tunnell went to the Madison County Courthouse in Anderson and took out a marriage license. One question on the license asked the husband-to-be how he would support his wife if he were not employed full-time. Ron Patty wrote "college gym." He was also working at Delco-Remy, while Carolyn was employed by the church's Mission Board and playing piano for "The Christian Brotherhood Hour."

That week was a big one for news in the world: On Tuesday was the coronation of Queen Elizabeth II in England. That same day the United States tested an atomic bomb in the Nevada desert seventy-five miles from Las Vegas that was seen in San Francisco (four hunded miles away) and felt in Los Angeles. In Korea armistice talks were under way to end fighting, while in Washington Senator Joe McCarthy was on his Red Hunt. But at the Tunnell home in Anderson at 412 Stuart Circle, all the attention was on getting the new bride ready for her wedding.

The wedding was held Friday, June 5, 1953, at the Park Place Church of God at 7 P.M. Escorting the bride down the aisle to give her away in marriage was Dr. John A. Morrison, president of Anderson College (Carolyn's father was the minister). It was a beautiful ceremony on the hot muggy evening. Candles, tied with white ribbons and flanked by palms, were lighted on each side of the altar. On the altar itself was a huge bouquet of white flowers and greenery and on each side of the front aisles were large single candles, while at the back of the church there was a seven-branched candelabrum on each side of the center aisle.

It was a wedding appropriately full of music—Carol Minkler played bridal selections on the organ, Patty Bray sang "Because," Marie Lien played two selections on violin, and the maid of honor, Joyce Hodges, sang "The Lord's Prayer." Carolyn, who looked resplendent in her gown of white Chantilly lace and organdy over taffeta with a halo of artificial flowers holding the veil on her head, carried a white Bible with Amazon lilies on it. The maid of honor and bridesmaids wore gowns of summer pastels and had flowers in their hair.

After the double-ring ceremony, the wedding party and guests went over to the Fellowship Hall on the Anderson campus for the reception. Baskets of flowers accented the evening as Ron and Carolyn cut the four-tiered wedding cake. A little later the couple left for their honeymoon in New York City. When they returned to Anderson, they set up housekeeping just a short walk from the campus.

Back at school in September, entering their junior year, Ron and Carolyn Patty continued their activities. In his last season on the gridiron, wearing number 19 in the black and orange colors of the Anderson Ravens, Patty was voted Most Valuable Player by his teammates and named honorary team captain, although the team suffered through a losing season again.

When the spring semester rolled around and the baseball team took the diamond, Ron missed a number of games because he was singing in the choir, which had a spring tour.

The choir, composed of forty voices, was headed by Professor Robert Nicholson, who served as organizer, chaperone, director, and companion. They traveled through seven states in a special bus and at each church where they sang they received money from a collection, which paid for most of the expenses. The rest of the expenses were met by the general college fund, which viewed the choir as a way to promote the college.

Among the songs performed were "The Day of Judgment," "Alleluia," "Ezekiel Saw de Wheel," "Let All the Nation Praise the Lord," and "A Mighty Fortress Is Our God." This was the first time Ron and Carolyn traveled together this extensively with the choir (the previous spring, on a jaunt through four states to fourteen Churches of God, Carolyn traveled while Ron played baseball) and this must have given them their first real taste of what would become their lifetime ministry—traveling and singing together in churches all over the United States.

Ron and Carolyn were both quite active on campus. Carolyn was involved in the Camarada Club and A Cappella Choir during her sophomore, junior, and senior years and with the Chromatic Club as a sophomore. Well known for her musical ability, she often served as the accompanist for the choir and chorus, as well as on "The Christian Brotherhood Hour" radio show. As a student, she came under the tutelage of Dr. Paul Breitwiser and noted, "He opened up to me the concept of playing with feeling, not just playing the notes."

Ron was active in the Sachem Club ("Sachem" is an Indian word for "leader"), the A Club, A Cappella Choir, president of the sophomore class, member of the yearbook staff, and was in Who's Who in College. He had switched his major to Bible studies in his second year, with a minor in music, and was already gaining a reputation for his involvement with religious organizations and activities that would overshadow (and eventually replace) his heroics in sports.

In the 1954–55 school year, Ron Patty did not play ball or finish the requirements for his degree, so when diplomas were handed out at the college commencement on June 13, 1955, Carolyn Tunnell Patty received hers, but Ron Patty did not; it would be twenty years before he finished the requirements and received his degree from Anderson College. (He finally received his bachelor of arts degree in 1975.)

The football team that season certainly could have used him—their record sank to 2–7.

6

Sandra Faye Patty was born on Thursday, July 12, 1956, in Oklahoma City, Oklahoma. The pregnancy had not been an easy one for her mother; Carolyn was traveling a great deal of the time, accompanying her husband, who was singing with the Christian Brothers Quartet. When she was about three months' pregnant, Carolyn began to suffer hard labor pains. The couple was in Chicago, in the middle of a tour for the quartet. In the early morning, as Chicago was just beginning to wake up, Carolyn felt as if she was going to have a miscarriage and, with a sense of urgency in her voice, asked her husband to pray for her. Ron quickly sat on the bed, hugged his wife closely, closed his eyes, and, with his muscles tensed, prayed for God to protect his wife and their unborn child. Before Ron said, "Amen," Carolyn's pains had stopped. The young couple considered it a miracle when Carolyn delivered the bouncing baby girl six months later on that hot July day.

When Sandi was born, the musical *Oklahoma!* was a big hit on Broadway and the *Billboard* charts for that week report that the original cast recording was in the top ten of the album chart. It is not hard to imagine Ron Patty singing songs from the hit musical during his visits to the hospital. One thing Ron *did* do when he looked at his young daughter was wonder if they would have a singing family group. That was a dream of Ron's—to have a family that would sing together. He sang tenor and Carolyn sang alto—maybe this little one would sing soprano?

Sandi was born during a time when America was undergoing vast changes musically. Elvis Presley's debut album, *Elvis Presley,* was number one on the album charts the week she was born. The official "birth" of rock 'n' roll had occurred in September 1955 when Bill Haley and the Comets reached the number one spot with "Rock Around the Clock" from the movie *The Blackboard Jungle.* Also in 1955, Sam Phillips at Sun Records was recording music by Jerry Lee Lewis, Carl Perkins, Elvis Presley, and Johnny Cash, all of whom would usher in the rock 'n' roll era.

But that musical world was still in transition when Sandi was born. In the top ten on the charts were albums by Frank Sinatra *(Songs for Swingin' Lovers),* Harry Belafonte *(Calypso),* Lawrence Welk *(Bubbles in the Wine),* and the Four Freshmen *(Four Freshmen and Five Trombones),* as well as original cast recordings for the musicals *My Fair Lady, Carousel,* and *Picnic.* The top song that week was "Wayward Wind" by Gogi Grant, followed by "I Almost Lost My Mind" by Pat Boone, "Moonglow Theme from *Picnic"* by Morris Stoloff, "Standing on the Corner" by the Four Lads, "I Want You, I Need You, I Love You" by Elvis Presley, "I'm in Love Again" by Fats Domino, "Ivory Tower" by Cathy Carr, "Born to Be with You" by the Chordettes, "On the Street Where You Live" by Vic Damone, and "Heartbreak Hotel" by Elvis. "Castles in Spain" by Michel Legrand and "Allegheny Moon" by Patti Page were also heard on the airwaves as the generation gap created by rock 'n' roll was widening quickly.

For Ron and Carolyn Patty, who grew up during the 1940s and early '50s in the golden age of radio and the era of the Big Band, the new music must have been a hard pill to swallow.

Within days of Sandi's birth, Elvis had appeared on television's "The Steve Allen Show" (he would sell ten million records this year) and two days after she was born Ronald Reagan appeared on "The General Electric Theater" in *Prosper's Old Mother.*

In the summer of 1957, Ron Patty and the other members of

the Christian Brothers Quartet went to a music workshop sponsored by Fred Waring at the Delaware Water Gap in Pennsylvania; this trip would lead to one of the biggest moments in Ron Patty's professional life.

Patty was singing tenor at the time with the quartet, along with members Paul Clausen (baritone), Ernie Gross (bass), and Doug Oldham (lead or second tenor); Carolyn Patty was the accompanist. The quartet appeared regularly on "The Christian Brotherhood Hour," a radio program sponsored by the Church of God and led by Doug's father, Dr. Dale Oldham, who served as speaker and host. The quartet was first formed in 1949 with original members Lowell Williamson, Homer Shower, Gene Dyer, and Doug Oldham. During this early time, the quartet did some recordings on the Tru-Tone label, which was also the label of the popular McGuire Sisters.

The Church of God viewed the radio program as an outreach and underwrote the efforts to put the show on transcriptions and send it out to radio stations. The program featured choirs, choruses, and accompanists, but the quartet was always the most popular musical feature, so it was a great feather in Ron Patty's cap to be selected to be a member of the quartet because it meant that millions out in radioland would hear him sing. These included not only audiences in the United States but in foreign countries as well. At that time, 141 stations worldwide carried the program; later that figure would extend to 400.

The Waring Music Workshop was geared for television and was held at a summer camp that had once been a boys' school. The group stayed in barracks-like quarters, with little more than beds and running water, and ate in a cafeteria-type arrangement in a large hall.

Fred Waring had a major impact on choral music during his time and with his group, the Pennsylvanians, was featured regularly on network radio and television for over twenty years. Born in Tyrone, Pennsylvania, Waring organized a group known as Waring's Collegians with his brother Tom at Pennsylvania State University. The group kept this name until 1922 when the name was changed to Waring's Pennsylvanians. He became one of the most popular performing groups on radio during the 1930s and in 1949 first appeared on television.

Fred Waring formed Shawnee Press in 1947 to publish his own and other composers' choral compositions; that same year he also established the Waring Music Workshop for choral conductors and performers. He created a distinctive choral sound through his "tone syllable system" which emphasized distinct enunciation with stress on full vowel sounds.

Waring was filled with good sound advice which he imparted to his students, such as "If people don't show up to hear you, reprimand yourself, not the people. They know what they like, and, if you aren't giving them something worth coming back for, you've failed." Waring also taught the maxim: "A good choir director never has a bad choir for long, and a bad choir director never has a good choir for long." Waring stressed not only sound but sight as well—costumes, props, movement, and other little touches that are important to an audience. Waring worked hard to make sure that a group would look good as well as sound good. These touches could make a relatively inexperienced group look professional and polished.

Doug Oldham suggested that the group go to the summer 1957 gathering with the reasoning that: "We've come along fine in radio, but TV is the coming medium, and I think Fred could help us." Ron, Paul, and Ernie agreed and they were off.

After they arrived, Oldham ran into Jack Best, Waring's rehearsal conductor, and told him about the quartet. Jack asked, "When are you going to let me hear you?" The next day they auditioned for Jack Best, who was impressed enough to call in Waring, who sat in front of the quartet while they sang several numbers. The one Fred liked best was "I Bowed on My Knees and Cried Holy" and, after the group had finished auditioning, came forward and asked, "Would you like to come with us?"

This was a big break for the small town group, but they did not accept immediately. "Give us some time to think it over," Ron Patty told Waring. Carolyn suggested, "I think we should pray about it." After the prayer, Doug, Paul, and Ernie all agreed to do it, but Ron was reluctant. First, he had personal reservations about being with a secular group (even a group as clean-cut as Waring's) and second, he was disappointed that Carolyn was not included in the offer (Waring had Mark Lowery play for them at the organ).

At the end of the workshop, Ron had still not made up his mind, and the group left without giving Waring an answer. About two weeks later, just before rehearsals were to begin for the fall tour, Ron agreed to be a part of the quartet with Waring. They were called the Glory Voices. The pay was not much—$150 a week, plus lodging—and they did not get paid at all during the two weeks of rehearsals. But at the end of rehearsals, they recorded an album for Capitol in New York, which provided some needed money before the tour began.

A couple of weeks after the first Sputnik was launched by the Soviets in the fall of 1957, President Eisenhower invited Waring and his group to entertain Queen Elizabeth and Prince Philip. This was Elizabeth's first visit to the United States since her coronation and Washington rolled out the red carpet for her. On the evening of the White House ball, the Glory Voices did not get to perform as a quartet, but they sang with the Glee Club. On one hand, this made them all a bit miffed, but when it was over the exposure gave them bragging rights that would last a lifetime.

The tour with Waring was a series of one-nighters all over the country on a Greyhound Scenicruiser and the headliners were Jeanne Steel, Gordon Goodman, Len Kranedonk, Eleanor Forgione, Frank Davis, Nancy Reep, Patty Beems, and Pley McClintock. The Glory Voices did three songs each night.

The four young men left Fred Waring when the bandleader signed to do the "Club Oasis" TV show, sponsored by the Oasis cigarette company. The guys, all being dedicated Christians with the Church of God, could not be part of a show sponsored by a product as sinful as cigarettes, so they returned home during the last week of December and resumed their role as the Christian Brothers Quartet, singing on "The Christian Brotherhood Hour." By that time, Paul Hart had replaced Paul Clausen as the baritone.

7

The Pattys moved from Oklahoma City to Phoenix, Arizona, when Sandi was two and a half. The last Sunday they were at the Oklahoma church was a special one for the Patty family because young Sandi was making her singing debut as a soloist. The song was "Jesus Loves Me" and she sang it in front of the congregation, stopping in the middle to say howdy to her grandma, who was seated in the audience.

In Phoenix, where she lived for the next ten years, Sandi began piano lessons with her mother from the big *John Thompson Book of Piano.* When she was five, Sandi sang at a mother-daughter banquet, accompanied by her mother on piano. Singing a medley of rain songs, Sandi would run behind a screen to change clothes and put on a different hat during the medley—a cute routine and one that showed an early love of performing before an appreciative audience.

Sandi's mother—who was so talented that she could have been a concert pianist—taught Sandi and her two younger brothers, Craig and Mike, piano lessons. Sandi remembers: "Mom made sure we at least spent enough time at the piano to know if we liked it or not." Sandi also remembers that her mother "was always there for us when we got home from school. She always had our lunches packed as we left in the morning. She always took us wherever we were supposed to go." Sandi adds affectionately, "God has given incredible ladies like my mom a wonderful mission because He thinks they can handle it."

While Mama Carolyn taught music to the children, Papa Ron concentrated on lyrics. Sandi remembers her father saying, "Make every minute of a song be worth something. You're singing to communicate words through music, so never let a sensitive song get too rhythmic or a happy song get too slow." Sandi also learned a lot from her dad's positive reinforcement: that nothing is ever as bad as it seems and that she should take pride in even the smallest things. He also encouraged her to learn all the vocal parts of a song, not just the "easy" soprano parts.

When Sandi was eight and her brothers Michael and Craig were six and three, respectively, they began singing together in a little trio called the Patty Kids. Ron Patty remembers that Sandi "was never interested in singing 'la-la-la' or other meaningless sounds" but instead always wanted "to sing with real words." He also remembers that his daughter "didn't play much with dolls because they couldn't respond with words."

Historically, the Church of God has placed much emphasis on the conversion experience, insisting that the true believer always knows the place, date, and time of his or her conversion because it is so dramatic and life-changing that it should remain permanently etched on his or her memory. The contemporary Christian culture also places much emphasis on this "born-again" experience and the Christian audience wants to know about each celebrity's and performer's conversion: How did it happen, why, what led to it, and who influenced them? There is often a premium put on the dramatic conversion—the rescue from drugs, booze, or even death, a life snatched from the jaws of Hell just in the nick of time by the saving grace of God—and this has always caused a bit of awkwardness for Sandi because, as she admits, "I have no emotional story to tell. There has been no one significant turnaround time in my life where I have been totally desperate and someone told me about Jesus."

Sandi relates the story of her commitment, which occurred on

July 12, 1964—her eighth birthday. "Although I was very young, I knew that something was missing in my life, and that was Jesus and all of the wonderful things that He could do for me. So . . . I gave my life to Jesus. Jesus was the best birthday present I have ever received." She goes on to admit, "There have been those times in my life when I thought I knew more than God did about what was best for me . . . I very quickly got put back on the right track."

Sandi's "conversion" came at a time when the country was trying to put itself back together after the assassination of John Kennedy. The death of Kennedy, on November 22, 1963, is an event remembered by almost everyone in the country who was alive at that time—most people remember exactly where they were and what they were doing when they heard the news from Dallas—and for a young child, it must have made a strong impression in terms of thinking about her own mortality. The fact that Kennedy had a daughter about the same age as Sandi must have also had a strong impact because a child can easily relate to another child their own age and, in this case, imagine what it would be like to lose a father. Being surrounded by a Christian family who was deeply involved in the church, the lesson was surely pointed out about "never knowing" when your time will come.

At the church in Phoenix, where her father was minister of music, Sandi remembers being involved in the children's choir and the rhythm band, singing and "putting on little pageants." With her father so active in the church, Sandi states, "There was always a lot of preparation going on around the house for what he was doing at the church."

In school, Sandi fondly remembers a teacher who had a profound impact on her life. Mrs. Pat Rabe instilled the love of music in her and Sandi readily admits that Mrs. Rabe was "most influential in terms of music." A stimulating teacher, Mrs. Rabe also provided a role model for young Sandi, who says, "I saw what an impact she had on me, so I thought, 'Well, I have a desire to teach

One of Sandi Patti's early publicity photos. (CENTER FOR POPULAR MUSIC)

Sandi (center, with arms outstretched to the side) as a member of the cheerleading squad for the Crawford High School Colts.

Sandi (middle row, seated far right) as a member of the play productions class during her senior year in high school.

Sandi (front row, third from right) on her high school volleyball team as a junior.

The Park Place Church of God, where Sandi attends church and where she took some of her college music courses. She did her earliest solo concerts here.

The Bill Gaither Trio: Gloria (center), Bill (on the right), and Gary McSpadden (on the left).

Singing with Jim Hamill
of the Kingsmen.

The first home—and first office—for Sandi and John at 530 Grand Avenue in Anderson, Indiana. Located just a few blocks from the college, this house is where the couple lived after their marriage in November 1978.

Sandi's first gold album, for *Live... More Than Wonderful,* was received during a special reception given by the Benson Company in Nashville. Also receiving gold albums were (front row, left to right): Greg Nelson, producer; David T. Clydesdale, arranger; Sandi; and Lanny Wolfe, writer of "More Than Wonderful." (Back row, left to right): John Barker, publisher, the Benson Company; Bob Clark, engineer; Ron Griffin, publisher, representing Gaither Music; John Helvering; Randy Cox, publisher, Meadowgreen Music; Ron Hostetler, publisher, representing New Spring Publishing; Bill Taylor, executive with the Benson Company; and Bob Jones, president of the Zondervan Music Group. (CENTER FOR POPULAR MUSIC)

With Lanny Wolfe, writer of "More Than Wonderful," which won Song of the Year honors at the 1984 Doves. Sandi is pregnant with Anna here as she poses for pictures backstage. (CENTER FOR POPULAR MUSIC)

too, and share what I've learned.' " This would be a guiding force when she chose her major in college.

Sandi's dad remembers Christmas 1963 when seven-year-old Sandi wanted a bicycle more than anything else. Ron and Carolyn managed to save enough to get the bike and hid it in the neighbor's garage. On Christmas morning, Sandi looked under the tree—and saw no bike. Ron says, "Her little face began to pucker although she was trying really hard to hide her disappointment." Then she saw the note in the package she had just unwrapped that said: GO LOOK IN THE NEIGHBOR'S GARAGE. Recalling that time, Dad says, "There never has been a standing ovation given Sandi that made her face light up like that new bike on that special Christmas."

It was probably one of the next two Christmases—1964 or 1965—that the Patty kids received Beatle wigs and baseball bats. (Ron notes, "We figured any well-balanced kids should be able to love music *and* sports.") Sandi quickly organized a singing group, wearing the wigs and using the Louisville Sluggers as guitars while standing on the table!

Sandi also remembers a very special Christmas when they were in Phoenix. It did not look as if they would be able to afford their annual trip back to Sapulpa, Oklahoma, to visit with her Grandma and Grandpa Patty and her many other relatives. As Christmas got closer, the mood around the Patty household got a little more glum—they would miss the snow as well as their friends and relatives. But a couple of days before Christmas, Ron Patty decided to load the family in the car and head out for Oklahoma—1,100 miles away. The Patty clan in Arizona did not let the Patty clan in Oklahoma know they were coming, so when the carload of Ron, Carolyn, Sandi, Michael, and Craig arrived on Christmas Eve, singing "Joy to the World," Grandma Patty thought it was just another group of carolers singing the spirit of the Christmas season. That notion was soon dispelled and hugs were dispensed while tears welled up in everyone's eyes.

The next morning, when the kids awoke, there were even some presents under the tree for them. Sandi wondered, "How did

Santa know we were going to be at Grandma Patty's house for Christmas?" Later she realized that her relatives had gotten some presents together and wrapped them up that night so that Christmas morning would be special. And it certainly was.

The Pattys lived in Phoenix for about ten years (Ron Patty had a television program there, "Songs Over the Desert") until around the time of Sandi's junior high school years, when they moved to San Diego and another Church of God.

Sandi attended Crawford High School in San Diego and was active with the Madrigals (she was the piano accompanist), the girls' choir, the volleyball team (they were 2–2 in Sandi's junior year when she was on the team), and on the cheerleading squad, where she was a "song leader." One of the most popular routines performed by the Crawford cheerleaders was a "striptease" in front of their fans. Special moments at Crawford include the Associated Student Body (ASB) Ball at the El Cortez Hotel and the ASB Ball when she was a senior at the Le Baron Hotel in the Regency Room with the theme "Our Night of Roses."

Sandi's senior year was filled with activities at school and church, as well as singing with the Ron Patty Family. Active in the play productions class, Sandi had a role in *Dark of the Moon,* as well as helping in another production, *Look Homeward, Angel.*

Musically, Sandi was influenced by two singers—Karen Carpenter and Barbra Streisand. Karen Carpenter had a string of hits during this time, including "Close to You," "We've Only Just Begun," and "Superstar," that caused young girls like Sandi to want to emulate her. Sandi says, "I didn't just want to *sing* like Karen Carpenter—I wanted to *be* Karen Carpenter!" She remembers getting Karen Carpenter songbooks, then sitting at the piano, where she would "sing the songs the way I thought Karen would sing them." She would also listen to albums by the Carpenters over and over, trying to learn the phrasing and get it just right.

By the time she became a senior, however, Sandi was "consumed" by the music and voice of Barbra Streisand and admits that Streisand's influence "has shaped so much of what I do now—the techniques I've tried to incorporate into my style." Sandi especially admired Streisand's phrasing. "One of the things about Barbra Streisand is that you always understand every word. That is something I learned from her—every word is there for a reason, so don't make any less of it."

In the middle of Sandi's senior year, the Carpenters' *The Singles 1969–1973* album was the top seller in the nation, followed by *Jonathan Livingstone Seagull* by Neil Diamond, and *Goodbye Yellow Brick Road,* by Elton John. When she graduated, the top song on the radio was "The Streak," by Ray Stevens and the Class of '74 was also hearing "Won't Last a Day Without You" by the Carpenters, "Haven't Got Time for the Pain" by Carly Simon, and "Band on the Run" by Paul McCartney and Wings.

Vacation time in the summers had always been a time for the Ron Patty Family to hit the road, with Ron booking concerts in churches between San Diego and Anderson as the family made their way back to the annual camp meeting for the Church of God in Anderson, Indiana. But by the time Sandi finished high school, Ron Patty had quit his job as minister of music with the church and gone full-time into traveling and singing. In essence, Sandi's career is following in the footsteps of her father and it is no wonder she spends so much time traveling—it is in her blood.

Reminiscing about her childhood, Sandi smiles and says, "I have the most wonderful parents in the world. I have such fond memories of my childhood . . . taking piano lessons with my mother and playing softball with my dad. My brothers tell me I was real bossy—that I'd make 'em play school, take tests, and everything." She adds, "I really wasn't a rotten kid. I had a messy room, but I got along with my parents and I enjoyed school."

Growing up in such a loving Christian environment made Sandi feel secure when the world around looked as if it was crumbling. During her senior year, the Watergate hearings were being conducted in Washington. Just before she left for college, Richard Nixon resigned in disgrace and, although the United States had withdrawn from Vietnam, the war there was still raging.

8

The year 1977 began with the coldest wave to hit the United States in over a hundred years. In Anderson, the snow was fifteen inches deep, the winds fifteen to twenty miles per hour, and the temperature hovered around the zero mark at the end of January. Jimmy Carter, the first "born-again" President, was sworn in and Christians were flexing their political muscles and realizing they had significant clout in that arena. But at the end of January, most Americans were huddled inside trying to keep warm while *Roots* was on television.

Those in Indiana had good reason to hold their heads high in the sports world, as Larry Bird was stinging the net for Indiana State, Notre Dame was on top in college football, and the Indianapolis 500 featured the first woman driver, Janet Guthrie, who, like the rest of the field, followed A. J. Foyt across the finish line.

The year would be a major one for the entertainment industry in general and gospel music in particular. This was the year Elvis Presley, Bing Crosby, Charlie Chaplin, and Groucho Marx died, the year Chuck Colson, Nixon's former hatchet man, would have a best-selling book, *Born Again,* and Debby Boone would have a number one pop hit with "You Light Up My Life." The daughter of 1950s teen idol Pat Boone, Debby would bring attention to gospel music because of her overt Christian beliefs and this song, which was not really a "gospel" song but could be interpreted that way.

It was also the year *Record World,* a music industry trade magazine, would publish a special section on gospel music. With this issue, gospel music came to the attention of the secular music industry. This would lead to long-term changes among retailers and other industry personnel that made gospel music more visible in the music industry overall. For the gospel industry itself, this would give it a boost in self-confidence and begin to make contemporary Christian music a major force both within the gospel world and the pop music world-at-large.

The gospel world in 1977 was all aglow over the first album on a Christian label to be certified gold. *Alleluia, a Praise Gathering for Believers,* by the Bill Gaither Trio on the Benson Company's record label, achieved this honor. It ushered in an era when gospel music would increasingly reach this plateau. Before this time, this was an untouchable dream, reserved for secular labels and nonreligious artists. Dominating the gospel world, in addition to the Bill Gaither Trio, were B. J. Thomas, Evie Tornquist, Andrae Crouch, Jimmy Swaggart, Reba Rambo Gardner, the Downings, Dallas Holm, Walter Hawkins and the Love Center Choir, James Cleveland, Jessy Dixon, and Danniebelle. Two albums that were released in 1977 had a major impact on the gospel music of the next few years. *For Him Who Has Ears* by Keith Green took the contemporary Christian music world by storm and Green soon emerged as a spiritual as well as musical leader in this movement. *Music Machine* by Candle would also reach gold status and lead the children's music movement, showing the gospel industry that there is a huge market for children's albums in the Christian culture.

It was a transitional year for gospel music and the Dove Awards reflected that. For the Doves, an annual awards show sponsored by the Gospel Music Association, it would mark the decline of the dominance of Southern gospel music among the award winners and the rumbles of what would be the major earthquake in gospel called "contemporary Christian music."

The Doves had their first awards show at the Peabody Hotel in Memphis on October 10, 1969. The idea of the awards had been suggested by Bill Gaither at a Gospel Music Association board of directors' meeting the previous year in Nashville. Les Beasley (head of the Florida Boys group), along with the help of a graphic artist, had created the design of the Doves. In that first year it was part of the Southern Gospel Quartet Convention (and would remain part of this annual October gathering until 1979) and the first winners came from the Southern gospel world. Among those carrying home awards that first year were the Oak Ridge Boys, J. G. Whitfield, Bill Gaither, Vestal Goodman, James Blackwood, the Imperials, and the Speers, while "Jesus Is Coming Soon" was named Song of the Year.

The Dove Awards were held in Memphis the first three years before moving to Nashville in 1972. Here, the Doves have been held in a giant tent over the plaza between the Capital Park Inn and Municipal Auditorium, the War Memorial Auditorium, the Ryman, Hyatt Regency Hotel, Opry House, Opryland complex, and Tennessee Performing Arts Center. The 1977 Doves were held at the Hyatt Regency in Nashville and featured a sit-down dinner, as well as the show and awards. Jim and Tammy Bakker created a stir when they appeared and carried home a Dove for Best Television Show for "The PTL Club"—which was only three years old at the time. Other winners that evening were the Cathedrals, the Speers, James Blackwood, Evie Tornquist, Bill Gaither, Henry Slaughter, the Couriers, the Blackwood Brothers, and "Learning to Lean" for Song of the Year.

But something else was happening in the fall of 1977 that would play a major role in gospel music and the Dove Awards—although it was happening about 350 miles away from Nashville and the Dove gathering. During the same month that the 1977 Doves were held, Sandi Patty was auditioning—and being accepted for—the group New Nature at Anderson College. It was in this group that she met her future husband and manager, John Helvering.

Christian colleges often have student musical groups who perform at other colleges and churches, promoting the college and the gospel. A number of groups had been formed at Anderson through the years—with names like Everyday People, Bright Day, and others—so New Nature came from a long tradition. Formed by Mick Guilliam, a music education major, and Don Kunselman, a broadcasting major, auditions were held with Dr. Dale Bengston of the music department and Mark Roller, director of admissions, sitting on the panel to make the final decisions. Students selected to sing were Guilliam, Kunselman, Cynthia Carey, Steven Justice, Daniel Marler, Harold Powell, Kathy Sells, Paul Thomas, John Helvering, and Sandi Patty.

The significance of this group was not in their musical performances—they played mostly soft middle-of-the-road easy-listening numbers geared for churches—but because this is where John and Sandi first met. Little did anyone know that this small group, which was disbanded and forgotten a year or so later, would plant the seeds for the team who would dominate church gospel music in the 1980s.

For Sandi, it was love at first sight when she met John. "I've always been in love with my husband," she said. "I've always been just crazy about him." The feelings, it soon became apparent, were mutual, and a romance was developing as the two college students began dating. New Nature would not really begin performing fully until spring 1978, but in the meantime there were choir rehearsals, classes to attend, chapel, and plenty of time for each other in an otherwise busy, hectic schedule.

Sandi went through some major changes during the time she was at Anderson—a process of maturing and finding herself—and her personal views were altered to those that were secure in a totally Christian environment. Obviously Sandi missed Southern California and she missed her family, but she was getting serious about her singing and about her personal life and she felt that Anderson College was where she should be.

Sandi first entered Anderson after she had graduated from

Crawford High School. But after one semester she quit and returned to Southern California to be with her family.

Back in San Diego, Sandi took classes at San Diego State and worked as a teaching assistant at a local junior high school while singing with her family. She was unwilling to break the ties to home, so she stayed with her family in San Diego, traveling around the country with them from church to church when the Ron Patty Family performed. But somehow she knew she would end up back at Anderson College—after all, this is where her parents went to school and the site of the annual camp meetings for the Church of God. The roots there were too deep to be denied and they pulled on her while she was attending San Diego State.

When Sandi re-enrolled at Anderson College in the fall of 1976, she began voice lessons with Greta Domenic in the music department and took it all very seriously. She had realized that the church world—the world of the Christian culture—was where she felt most comfortable, though she had been to a secular high school and had idolized the pop talents of Karen Carpenter and Barbra Streisand. She still admired and respected Streisand's voice, and worked hard to achieve that same discipline and control, but she felt more comfortable singing church songs rather than torch numbers. She felt she would be singing her whole life and wanted to do it right, although she tended to think of herself in terms of a music teacher who would do some solo performances on the side, or be involved in the church choir—maybe even still sing with her family sometimes—rather than as a full-time performer.

It was during 1977 that Sandi began to go to Pinebrook Studio to sing on sessions. Whenever someone in the Anderson area can sing well in the studio, word gets around quickly. The pool of talent is not as large as, say, Nashville, Los Angeles, or New York, so word spread among the engineers and producers at Pinebrook that Sandi Patty was a great singer and she was called upon often. She spent a lot of time in front of the microphone in the studio there, gaining valuable studio experience.

The key elements to being a good studio singer have as much

to do with personality as with talent: The person must work quickly in the studio, getting along with a variety of different personalities (often with a large share of individual quirks). The singer must also be adaptable, so that no matter what style is required he or she grasps it quickly and sings it in a convincing manner. The person must be able to read arrangements as well as pick up something by ear, hearing a part and singing it without a great deal of rehearsal. And, through all this, the singer must remain amicable, tolerant, and polite, keeping a pleasant demeanor and subtle sense of humor so they can roll with the punches. It is a demanding business with a lot of pressure; only those with grace under pressure and a unique talent can pull it off. Sandi Patti is one of those people and her friendliness and talent were a potent combination—it was how she earned her way through college.

Sandi has said of her studio work: "I was able to practice for two years and was paid for it. In the studio, I had to sing like so many different people. It helped me prepare for what I'm doing now—switching from one style of music to another."

Those who worked with Sandi from those days remember her as an incredible talent and one of the nicest people they ever met. One engineer remembers: "After a busy day in the studio, she always made it a point to personally thank everyone who had anything to do with the recording and later send that person a letter of thanks."

9

The Christian culture witnessed some significant developments during the mid-1970s as Christian bookstores grew at an astounding rate. The Christian Booksellers' Association began in 1950 with 25 stores; in 1986 there were about 3,500 member stores and about 5,500 overall. In 1971 these stores were bringing in an estimated $100 million annually in revenue, by 1976 that figure had jumped to $500 million, and in 1985 that figure was $1.3 billion or an average of $235,000 per store.

The "me-decade," as journalist Tom Wolfe described the 1970s, was becoming the "we-decade" for the Christian community as they began to voice an "us versus them" mentality when they fought for issues such as prayer in schools, anti-abortion measures, and creationism rather than Darwin's theory of evolution to be taught in schools. It was the beginning of a movement that would market Christianity in a way it had never been marketed before. The Christian bookstores provided a network to sell Christian books and records (this would benefit Sandi Patti immensely a few years later because this is where most of her records would be sold).

The secular media provided more coverage on the Christian movement and the Christian media developed at an astounding rate. Evangelists discovered television in a big way after the Federal Communication Commission altered its ruling on public service for the airwaves and cable television began to grow and be accepted in American homes.

The Christian culture cannot be underestimated in America—it accounts for billions of dollars of revenue, creates its own celebrities, and has its own marketing network with the Christian bookstores. It has saturated the market through all the media: radio, television, books, periodicals, prerecorded music, and videos. It has also created its own alternative culture: It is possible for someone to be educated in Christian schools his whole life—from preschool through college, receive Christian periodicals in his home, buy Christian books, play Christian music on his stereo, watch Christian programs on his television, work for a Christian company, and be involved in Christian organizations in his off-hours. The church provides the center for social activity and a source of friends—so an individual immersed in this culture may have little contact with nonbelievers in his daily life.

The most visible examples of the Christian culture are the televangelists, but they give a distorted view of the culture: There are only a relative handful of these people dominating this field and their success—bringing in hundreds of millions of dollars each year—is out of proportion to the rest of the culture, which is basically a middle-class phenomenon.

This period—1976–77—also laid the groundwork for the Republican Revolution led by Ronald Reagan. This brought him to the presidency in the 1980 election and caused the word "liberal" to be taboo while everyone clamored to be labeled "conservative," a reversal of the political in-word vocabulary of the late 1960s and early 1970s.

It was Winston Churchill who once said, "Anyone who is not a liberal when they are twenty has no heart; and anyone who is not a conservative when they are forty has no brain." Considering that quote, it must be asked: Was the generation of college students in the late 1970s without a heart or did they just learn quickly and get smart early? Since the college days generally lay the groundwork for the attitudes, interests, and involvements for the rest of a person's life, it is enlightening to look at the prevailing attitudes of college students in general during the time John Helvering and Sandi Patty were undergraduates at Anderson College.

Studies of this group of students show a pronounced shift toward conservatism in voting registrations (a large number registered as Republicans) but an overall political apathy on campuses during this time. There was a continuing trend toward "me-ism" and a lack of concern for political activism: Let's stick to the basics, get government out of the individual's life (and hence concern about government), and concentrate on personal success, getting rich, and being elitist. This is perhaps expressed best in the "average" college student of this time, who registers as a Republican, is very materialistic, wants less government regulation and intrusion, while having lots and lots of success and recognition.

In a study conducted by the Cooperative Institutional Research Program of UCLA in the early 1980s, there appeared to be some major differences between students at religious schools and their secular counterparts. For instance, the religious college student tended to view himself as "conservative," was less likely to drink beer or smoke, and more likely to be against abortion, couples living together outside marriage, premarital sex, and homosexuality. These students tended to be higher achievers than the secular college students and more involved with extracurricular activities, although they were more likely to take tranquilizers, according to this survey.

Overall, these college students of the late 1970s and early 1980s said that raising a family was more important than influencing social values and that "getting a job" was the primary reason for going to college (as oppossed to "preparing graduates for a life of involved and committed citizenship"). Over 80 percent of this group received financial support for college outside the home (thus allowing their parents more affluence), while a whopping 94 percent were bored in class.

Another survey, comparing the college students of 1969–70 with the 1977–78 students, described the latter group as "more career oriented, better groomed, more concerned with material success, more concerned with self, and more practical," adding that the 1977–78 students were "less radical, less activist, and less hostile."

Clearly, this generation of college students demonstrated a major turn away from societal concerns and toward inner, personal concerns. A large part of the explanation is that these students grew up during a time of disillusionment with the political system as they witnessed the ravages of an unjust war in Vietnam, the scandal of Watergate, and resultant loss of prestige in the presidency caused by the resignation of Richard Nixon, as well as numerous other scandals that brought dishonor (and even jail sentences) to political leaders. Most in this generation rejected social/political concerns and became caught up in a "me-ism."

Many—especially within the Christian culture—considered the rise of "me-ism" a major factor in the rise of the Christian movement that swept the country in the mid-1970s to mid-1980s as people saw the church as a way to draw closer together to others. The conservative movement that developed hand in hand with Christian revivalism provided a new kind of activism for this generation whose overriding concern was personal success and provided the answer most asked by this generation: What's in it for *me?*

Although Sandi Patti has been modestly involved in World Vision and participated in "Do Something Now," the Christian answer to "We Are the World," it is obvious that, like most of the rest of her generation, she is not preoccupied with political concerns. In the end, this may be a strength for her relating to her audience because she fits so well within her generation and the Christian culture as a whole.

At any rate, politics was definitely not on Sandi's mind at the end of the 1977 semester, but a young man named John Helvering definitely *was.* They were both members of the Anderson College choir at this time and as they sat in the Park Place Church of God for the annual "Candles and Carols" service, Sandi thought about the fall semester and the new young man in her life. As the choir and congregation sang "Silent Night," the darkened chapel was illuminated by one lone candle, held by Anderson College president Robert Reardon, who lit another's candle, who in turn lit the candle of the one next to him.

A little earlier, the choir, along with the Wind Ensemble and the Anderson Symphony Orchestra (all under the direction of Dr. Eugene Miller), had performed Shaw-Bennett's "The Many Moods of Christmas," Trudi Fulda had performed a solo of a Caribbean folk carol, "Mary's Little Boy Child," and Dean Robert Nicholson had lead a responsive reading from the New Testament. Now it was time of quiet reflection; Sandi sat holding her candle, singing.

When the week of Christmas arrived, there was further proof that the Christian culture was a major movement: Jesus was on the cover of *Time.*

10

It was a cold, cold winter filled with ice and snow when Sandi Patty and John Helvering began classes in late January 1978. It was a busy time for them with choir practice, rehearsals for New Nature, and Sandi performing solo at some events—plus the usual round of classes with their requisite papers, exams, and reports.

On February 24 Sandi presented "An Evening with Sandi" at Byrum Hall on the Anderson campus. The concert was sponsored by Amici and featured "sacred and secular" music during the two Friday evening performances. Also, in late February, Sandi performed at a Little Siblings Weekend for relatives of Anderson students who were between the ages of six and eighteen. Created by the Student Activities Department (SAD), the program featured ventriloquist Mary Mathis, as well as films, recreation, a variety show, and an ice cream social. Already, during this time, Sandi was showing her love for performing for children.

The choir tour lasted from March 24 to April 2 and covered four states. John and Sandi were among the sixty choir members (Sandi sang soprano; John sang tenor) led by Dr. Eugene Miller. The choir performed music by Bernstein, Mendelssohn, and Handel, as well as various anthems, hymns, and spirituals in their repertoire. The tour—the thirty-third such event since the choir began in 1945—began with a 1 P.M. performance at Chanute Air Force Base

Chapel in Rantoul, Illinois, with another performance that evening at the People's Church of God in Decatur, Illinois.

The first Easter John and Sandi spent together was in 1978 and on that rainy Sunday they performed with the choir at a morning service in St. Louis and an evening concert in De Soto, Missouri. Like so many holidays to come, this one would be spent traveling to a performance and their memories would hold a mixture of setting up for a concert and performing, as well as spending a special time together.

Earlier that semester New Nature had given their first concert at the Park Place Church of God after the church chili supper. It was a good warm-up for the tour scheduled that summer, but the group was put on "hold" until after the choir returned from the spring break tour. When they did resume, it was at a special three-day rehearsal camp held at Marengo, Ohio, in late May before they made their summer tour debut performance in Indianapolis. During the following two weeks before the International Convention of the Church of God in Anderson, the group performed in thirteen Churches of God in Indiana, Ohio, and Pennsylvania.

Pictures of Sandi during this time show her with a short haircut, boyishly styled, with a part on the left. John had an Afro that encircled his head like a huge brown sphere.

John and Sandi both thrived on the bustle of the spring 1978 semester: Both loved singing and traveling, but most of all they found they enjoyed each other. It was a time that would bind them to Anderson College as they plunged headlong into school activities and classes. No longer did Sandi have a shortage of friends. Each day more people at Anderson College became aware of this young lady and her singing talent.

Being a church-related school (with 60 percent of the students coming from a Church of God background) meant that every Tuesday and Thursday morning at 10 A.M. all full-time students were required to attend chapel, where there was singing, worship, and then a guest speaker or lecture. The close ties between church and school rankled some—one eighteen-year-old freshman felt that church "stifled" her self-expression, but another student, a graduating senior, stated, "I like it here with the church's influence. I came for a Christian education." A third student stated he was "surprised to find the system so educationally open, considering the tie between the church and school."

Graduation time at Anderson in 1978 would not bring Sandi a diploma, but it would bring her some recognition. The eighty-ninth annual International Convention of the Church of God, which began with the college commencement on June 19, would find even more people becoming aware of Sandi's talent through her performances with New Nature. This week-long gathering would play host to approximately twenty-five thousand people (including thirty missionaries from a dozen nations) who would congregate on the church's grounds east of Anderson College and participate in three hundred scheduled conferences, institutes, workshops, seminars, and other special programs. This particular convention would have a central focus on "mission" work.

At the commencement, Robert Reardon, president of the college, made a special plea for women in the church, stating, "The doors to ministry for women in the church have been closed by our prejudice long enough. Among our young women are bright minds, sensitive hearts, that represent one of the great untapped resources for the church. God is not only calling them, but today—now—He is calling us to have done with our narrowness and blindness and open our arms to the ministry of women."

Reardon also admonished the graduates: "Don't play the world's dreariest game—Follow the Leader. Take charge of your own life. Trust in the Lord with all your heart; take a deep breath and plunge in . . . I have little doubt that you are made of good stuff."

For Sandi Patty, there must have been a few bittersweet thoughts—this is the year she was supposed to have graduated, but she would have to wait another year to receive her diploma. On the other hand, this was becoming the most exciting year of her life—she was singing and performing in numerous concerts all over the place and spending her time in the company of a young man she was wild about.

During convention week, New Nature performed nine concerts in six days. In addition to singing, the group did dramatic readings, puppetry, and a computerized slide show.

New Nature had recorded an album at Pinebrook Studio that spring and it was available during the Church of God convention. Group members were excited about selling the records and cassettes when they were on the road that summer. The primary purpose of the group was to "disseminate a religious message through music and inform others about Anderson College," according to cofounder Don Kunselman. This promotion of the college is the reason the school paid for the recording of the album and made it available through their admissions office. Group members Kunselman, Mick Gilliam, Paul Thomas, Dan Marler, Cindi Carey, Steve Justice, Kathy Sells, Bucky Powell, John Helvering, and Sandi Patty had enjoyed recording the easy-paced contemporary Christian material.

Leaving Anderson at the end of June, the group spent seven weeks performing at churches, youth camps, a drama and music camp, a college, and, finally, at the Church of God youth convention held that summer in Seattle. The seventeen-state tour, sponsored by the school's Student Summer Service Program, was part of Anderson College's annual summer outreach that sent over four hundred students out all over the world to take part in service projects.

11

In July 1978 a new magazine, which was geared to contemporary Christian music, appeared. *Contemporary Christian Music* began as a music tabloid, based in Santa Ana, California, and during the first year twelve thousand copies of each issue were mailed for free each month to those involved in the gospel music industry. On that first cover were Pat Boone's daughters, who had recorded an album for their father's label, Lamb & Lion Records. This magazine would dominate the contemporary Christian field, becoming the most popular and influential magazine in that area. Within that first year, in fact, it became to contemporary Christian music what *Rolling Stone* is to rock—*the* publication that defined a music culture and identified who's in and who's not.

Contemporary Christian Music—or *CCM,* as it is called—actually began as a tabloid paper called *Contemporary Christian Acts* in Orange County, California. The paper was owned primarily by Jim Willems, who also owned the Maranatha Village Christian bookstore, which was responsible for selling more contemporary Christian albums than any other store in the country. The music editor for *Acts* was John Styll, a radio disc jockey who had been the host of the Calvary Chapel Saturday night radio concerts and was doing some syndicated shows at the time. Since the music section of *Acts* was so popular, it was decided to make John Styll editor of the new publication.

The group owning and editing *CCM* attended Calvary Chapel in Southern California, so the magazine had an obviously West Coast slant. Also, it saw itself geared to rock 'n' roll gospel, since that was the stronghold of that music. However, in their charts, they had "inspirational" and "Southern gospel" in addition to "rock."

The charts of *CCM* were a major contribution to contemporary Christian music because no other publication compiled charts from Christian bookstores about music, which is where most of the Christian buyers bought their records. The only other gospel music charts during this time were in *Record World,* and these were compiled primarily from secular distributors who handled some gospel product as part of their normal business. Thus, they showed more sales on Southern gospel and black gospel, which are sold primarily through regular retail outlets, rather than the fledgling contemporary Christian music, which had to depend upon the Christian bookstore to reach its core audience.

Those first charts in *CCM* were compiled from about twenty-five Christian bookstores for albums and sixty or seventy radio stations for airplay. The top song on that first chart for contemporary Christian music was "He's Alive" by Don Francisco, followed by "Old Man's Rubble" by Amy Grant, "All Day Dinner" by Reba, "Mansion Builder" by 2nd Chapter of Acts, "What a Difference You've Made in My Life" by Amy Grant, "Now I See the Man" by Chris Christian, "Don't Look Back" by Fireworks, "First Butterfly" by the Boones, "Rise Again" by Dallas Holm, and "Building Block" by Noel Paul Stookey. Other artists on the airplay chart were Scott Wesley Brown, the Bill Gaither Trio, Steve Camp, the Archers, the Phil Keaggy Band, Farrell and Farrell, Stephanie Booshada, Karen Lafferty, Evie, and B. J. Thomas.

The top album in the contemporary category was *Mansion Builder* by 2nd Chapter of Acts, followed by *For Him Who Has Ears to Hear* by Keith Green, *Home Where I Belong* by B. J. Thomas, *How the West Was One* by 2nd Chapter of Acts, a Band Called David and the Phil Keaggy Band, *The Lady Is a Child* by Reba, *Forgiven* by Don

Francisco, *Emerging* by the Phil Keaggy Band, *Fresh Surrender* by the Archers, *Sweet Music* by the Pat Terry Group, and *Chance* by Chris Christian. On the inspirational album chart, the top album was *Mirror* by Evie, followed by two other albums from this young lady—*A Little Song of Joy for My Little Friends* and *Gentle Moments*—then *Live* by Dallas Holm, *Pilgrim's Progress* by the Bill Gaither Trio, *Praise II* by Maranatha! Music, *Praise Strings* by Maranatha! Music, *Come Bless the Lord* by the Continental Singers, *Praise Strings II* by Maranatha! Music, and *The Music Machine* by Candle.

The top sellers in contemporary Christian music were B. J. Thomas and Evie Tornquist; each was selling over 100,000 units of each release and some albums by these artists reached the 3–400,000 plateau. But for most acts, sales of 20,000 were considered good for a first album and 40,000 units was a hit.

In October *Record World* published its second "Gospel Music Special" and named the top sellers in contemporary and inspirational music for the past year. Heading the list was *Mirror* by Evie, followed by *Home Where I Belong* by B. J.Thomas, *Gentle Moments* by Evie, *For Him Who Has Ears to Hear* by Keith Green, *Alleluia, a Praise Gathering for Believers* by the Bill Gaither Trio, *Praise II* by Maranatha! Music, *Live* by Dallas Holm and Praise, *This Is Not a Dream* by Pam Mark, *Live from Nashville* by Jimmy Swaggart, and *The Music Machine* by Candle. Others on the list of top sellers included Mike Warnke, Reba Rambo Gardner, Andrae Crouch, Joe Reed, the Phil Keaggy Band, 2nd Chapter of Acts, Seawind, and J. D. Sumner and the Stamps (with their tribute to Elvis album).

The 1978 Dove Awards were held at the Opryland Hotel. Dallas Holm was the big winner that night, carrying home four Doves, including Song of the Year honors for "Rise Again." He also won the Songwriter of the Year award, becoming the first person other than Bill Gaither to win the honor since the inception of the Doves. Evie was Female Vocalist for the second year in a row and the Imperials were the top group. Other award winners were Dino Kartsonakis, the Cruse Family (for Contemporary Album of the Year with their *Transformation* album), the Bill Gaither Trio, the

Boones, Andrae Crouch, and the Blackwood Brothers. George Beverly Shea and Mahalia Jackson were inducted into the Gospel Hall of Fame.

This was another critical year for the Gospel Music Association and the Dove Awards because new blood was being infused—in the form of Dallas Holm, Evie, and Dino Kartsonakis—while some of the old-timers were being eased out. In June of that year, the GMA had signed an agreement with a Hollywood-based production firm to televise the Doves for the first time, but no deal could be struck and the show was not televised. That year the GMA also announced a $1.5-million building across from the Country Music Hall of Fame to house the Gospel Music Hall of Fame, offices, and a Research Center. But the money could not be raised and that area gave rise to the Barbara Mandrell Museum and Store.

In the music world, 1978 began with the ill-fated American tour of the Sex Pistols. This group would not last, but the punk movement would have an impact on fashion as well as music and lead another British invasion into American pop music. The Grammy Awards on February 15 gave Barbra Streisand her first Grammy in twelve years (for "Evergreen"—the theme from the movie *A Star Is Born)* and honored Debby Boone as Best New Artist. There were only three categories for gospel that year and B. J. Thomas won for Inspirational Performance, the Happy Goodman Family won for Traditional Gospel Performance, and Larry Hart took home the Grammy for Contemporary Gospel Performance.

The Hart win shocked the gospel industry—he was a virtual unknown who had recorded a custom album—and his win was the basis for some major changes in the Grammy voting process. Hart's victory came after he had signed up the members of the choir in his father's church in Detroit and bloc-voted for the award. The scandal cast a cloud over the Grammys but, in the end, gospel music benefited from the increased attention. The Grammy telecast featured more performances by gospel artists and the number of categories would increase dramatically in the 1980s.

Already, the NARAS (National Academy of Recording Arts and Sciences) board of directors was beginning to recognize gospel music as a more significant part of America's music; the previous year there had only been two categories for gospel music—inspirational (won by Gary S. Paxton for his album *The Astonishing, Outrageous, Amazing, Incredible, Unbelievable, Different World of Gary S. Paxton)* and gospel performance (other than soul), which was won by the Oak Ridge Boys.

Overall, though, the musical world of 1978 was dominated by the Bee Gees with "Stayin' Alive" and other songs from the *Saturday Night Fever* soundtrack. By the end of the year, it was estimated they had sold more records in the past twelve months than the entire gospel music field combined.

12

When John and Sandi returned to school in September 1978, they were deeply in love and planning their wedding for later that fall. Time spent together on the road had nurtured the spark and fanned it into a full-grown flame. Already their courtship had set the pattern for what their married life would be—traveling and performing all across the country, John taking care of business details and the sound system, Sandi singing before crowds who were awed by her talent.

When they had first talked about marriage, they had thought of what it would be like when Sandi was a music teacher and John was an accountant. But this talk was just a diversion, an attempt to construct some "reality" in their future plans. From the very first, John saw in Sandi not only the love of his life but a powerful singer and he saw how people reacted when she sang. He also knew how much Sandi loved to sing and how much performing was part of her essential makeup (she still sang with her family whenever she could). Sandi did not really want to ever give up performing for audiences although, being "practical," she wanted something to "fall back on" as she prepared for the future—and teaching music in high school fit perfectly. Like her father, who had held a job as minister of music and still performed at other churches, Sandi felt she could hold the job of music teacher and still do her performing when she did not have to be at work.

When school began on September 5, there was a brand-new building for students taking music classes. The Fine Arts Building was partially open, giving students in music and art a new home with modern facilities. Previously, Sandi's music classes had been held in the church facilities at the Park Place Church of God.

Sandi performed her first solo concert that semester just after school started. She played the piano and sang; John was there to take care of the sound system and other details. This pattern would continue all fall.

It was also during this time that Sandi recorded her first solo album. Back in the wintery days earlier in the year when the streets were icy and slick, a car had slid into Sandi's car, which was parked on the side of the road. Nobody was hurt and—to Sandi's great relief—the driver was insured. Since her car still ran fine (although it looked a little ragged), Sandi kept driving it and pocketed the money from the insurance company. This money would be the budget for her first album, which was recorded up the road in Alexandria.

This first album would be life-changing in more ways than one. It was composed entirely of Sandi's solo efforts and it deepened the professional as well as personal relationship between John and Sandi because it was John who encouraged Sandi to do the album and supported her efforts throughout. Finally, it was the reason her name was changed from Patty to Patti.

The change in name came about because of a printer's error on the cover of the album. Rather than return the albums and have the printing done all over again or try to explain to buyers that the last name should end in *y* instead of *i,* Sandi just changed her name. She talked it over with her parents first, of course, and they did not mind the change. Sandi was getting married soon and thought she would have a new last name anyway. Thus, the girl with two first names became a name to remember.

That album was a big event in Sandi's life, but the biggest event that fall happened in November when she married her sweetheart, John Leonard Helvering, Jr.

John was born on October 13, 1954 in Houston, Texas, but came to Anderson when he was six months old with his family. He spent his school days in Anderson and graduated from Anderson High School. His father, John Helvering, Sr., was born in Bradford, Arkansas, and his mother, Doris Ophelia Helvering, was born in Raville, Arkansas. When John and Sandi met, he was a business major at Anderson College, planning to follow in his father's footsteps and become a CPA.

In the ensuing years, John and Sandi would usually spend the day of the Dove Awards in Nashville getting ready for that event, going through rehearsals and meetings with top people in the gospel music world. But on the day of the Dove Awards in 1978, John and Sandi went to Dr. Peter Szumilas for the medical examination they needed to obtain their marriage license.

The wedding took place Friday evening, November 17. John's parents came in from their home in Lake Wales, Florida, and Sandi's parents were in from San Diego for the event. In the tradition of her parents' wedding, the pastor officiating at the ceremony was the bride's father—Ron Patty—who joined the young couple in holy matrimony with a great deal of emotion on that cool rainy evening.

This was a week of big events, but one incident—a phone call—had to be shunted aside because of the hectic household filled with wedding plans.

Mike Cowart, an executive with Singspiration, the music division of the Zondervan Company, called Sandi Patti and told her he had a copy of her custom album, *For My Friends,* and would like to talk with her about signing a recording contract with his label. Cowart had received a copy of the album from David T. Clydesdale, a friend of Sandi's who is a songwriter, arranger, producer, and who had helped on the custom album.

Sandi politely told Cowart that she was happy to receive his call but that she was getting married on Friday and—first things first—she felt that landing a husband was more important than landing a record deal so could he please call back. When he called again, around the middle of January, a meeting was set up to discuss the future recording career of Sandi Patti.

The rest of 1978 was spent finishing classes at Anderson and getting adjusted to married life in the wooden frame house on the top of a hill just a few blocks from campus. Sandi's mother had told her when she was growing up, "When you marry someone, you really don't know him." Sandi's reaction had been, "Oh, Mother, that can't possibly be true." As 1978 drew to a close, she was learning her mother was right as she and John began to know each other as husband and wife.

That first Christmas was a most special time for Sandi who, for the very first time in her life, went Christmas shopping for her *husband.* In Anderson, Indiana, the weather favored young romantics on Christmas day, as snow flurries fell.

13

As 1979 got under way, Sandi Patti's job as a studio singer kicked into high gear. She was making regular trips up the road to Alexandria to sing at either Pinebrook Studio or the Barn. Sandi was successful here, singing jingles for Juicy Fruit gum, Steak-N-Shake, Indiana Bell telephone, the Ohio State Fair, and others.

The spring semester was, as usual, packed with activity for Anderson College students. To celebrate Black History Month, the Reverend Jesse Jackson spoke before four thousand students and New Nature performed for a vesper service at Park Place. B. J. Thomas, one of the top acts in contemporary Christian music at the time, appeared in concert at Anderson High School. Bringing Thomas (and opening act Steve Camp) to Anderson was the dream of two Anderson College students, Steve and Sandi Weishrod, and was the highlight of the year for contemporary Christian music followers. The concert was packed.

The meetings with Singspiration had gone well and when the Anderson College commencement arrived on June 19, life was looking rosy for Sandi. A lot of dreams had come true for her in the preceding year—she had toured the country with New Nature, she had married John, she had a recording contract with a major Christian company, and, at the end of the evening, she had a college diploma.

Sandi was among 429 students who received their awards that

evening of Anderson's sixty-first commencement. The commencement speech was given by Indiana Senator Richard Lugar, who spoke on some national and world issues, saying, "The United States of America may have to make very difficult choices of how we allocate our surpluses to which countries," alluding to the food for fuel controversy then being discussed, before urging students to be "sensitive" about some of the things which have been "taken for granted," concluding that it is "God's charge to us."

Sandi's degree, a bachelor of arts, was inscribed to "Sandra Faye Patty Helvering."

At the time of Sandi's commencement, Evie Tornquist had three albums on the inspirational/MOR chart in *CCM,* while the Bill Gaither Trio had five. Danny Gaither also had an album in the top twenty-five—which meant that the little area around Anderson, Indiana, provided the talent for almost a fourth of that chart. On the contemporary chart, Keith Green, B. J. Thomas, and Dallas Holm each had two albums in the top ten, while Amy Grant's first album was at number thirteen. On the Southern gospel charts, Jimmy Swaggart had three of the top eight albums.

Top songs on the inspirational/MOR chart were "I Am Loved" by the Bill Gaither Trio, "Rise Again" by Dallas Holm, and three from the Imperials: "Praise the Lord," "Oh, Buddah," and "Sail On." On the contemporary charts, "Blame It on the One I Love" by Kelly Willard was number one.

About a month after her graduation, Sandi made a very important appearance—she sang at the Christian Booksellers' Convention. The CBA Convention, as it is called, is a five-day gathering where the companies that produce Christian books, records, gifts, music, trinkets, and other assorted products gather to unleash all the might they can muster in order to obtain orders from Christian retailers. Over eight thousand attended the thirtieth annual trade show, with buyers from over sixteen hundred Christian bookstores placing orders. Built around the theme "Making Christ Known," the convention featured seminars as well as sales pitches, with topics that included "How to Sell the Top Ten Bibles," "Increasing

Sales with Specials and Promotions," "Displaying and Selling Music," "Store Personnel Management," and "Cash Flow Controls."

Sandi's performance during the CBA Convention in St. Louis created quite a stir and word soon spread throughout the convention that Sandi Patti is "a talent to watch."

She appeared at an artist showcase arranged by her label, Singspiration, and met some of the Christian bookstore personnel who would hopefully stock and sell her music. It was a good way to be seen, heard, and noticed by the people who count in the Christian retailing industry, and Sandi made a strong, positive impression with her first performance and appearance.

The first notice of Sandi's debut album came in the form of a full-page four-color ad in the October 1979 issue of *CCM,* which announced a "special introductory price" of $5.95 for the album. In the ad was the picture of Sandi that was used on the cover of the album. (Later this picture would be replaced by a picture of piano keys when the album was re-released.)

Already some key factors were beginning to emerge in the career of Sandi Patti that would have a long-range impact. First, she works hard on her career and is not afraid of self-promotion. Many artists in gospel music suffer from a professional schizophrenia: They want to be successful, but do not want to strive for it. They want to have top-selling albums, but are reluctant to use the tools of promotion and publicity. They want to be well-known to record buyers and concertgoers, but are hesitant to pursue "fame."

The psyche of those involved in Christian music as recording artists and performers is fragile and vacillates in their efforts to be "in" this world but not "of" it. They must be ministers, yet they must be entertainers too because they are in the arena of public performance. But they must not look at themselves too much as "entertainers," even when deep down they know that this is an important part of their performance. They are recognized—or want to be known—as "stars" and celebrities but also tell audiences (as well as themselves) that they are just ordinary people and perhaps the lowest of the lowly. On one hand, those in gospel music must have the giant ego required to go onstage night after night, yet be the humblest of the humble. And they may want all the major awards and gold albums for their wall, but must "reject" earthly success and the temptations of fame—all the while pursuing it.

Many artists feel they cannot achieve the success they pursue because it implies they are no longer what they say they are—lowly ministers serving Jesus. This spiritual side causes problems because on one hand they are supposed to be spiritual leaders and while they do spend most of their time onstage espousing their spirituality, offstage they find themselves dealing with day-to-day issues and having a greater interest in their music than in being some sort of pastor-in-concert.

All of this emanates from a cornerstone in American Christianity—guilt. Guilt gnaws at Christian performers because too often they are not what they say they are. By trying to please Christian audiences, their musical peers, attain a perceived ideal of what a Christian should be, and answer to their own inner drives and ambitions, artists feel many forces pulling against each other. Topping off all this, of course, is God Himself, who seems to stand over Christian artists with both a whip and loving arms, constantly reprimanding and forgiving, demanding perfection but lovingly accepting much less.

An element which would emerge in Sandi's career is the insistence of "quality" on everything with her name attached to it. The advertisement should be full-page, in color, and it should feature her in the best possible light. All pictures should be flattering, all stories should be positive, and all her albums should have the very best songs with the very best production. These are Sandi's demands on herself and those around her.

Sandi has never been adverse to spending her own money as an investment in her career—she has not depended upon the record company or anyone else to think of the idea of buying ads—she and John have often done that themselves. The ads have always been graphically sleek and appeared in top publications. She has never been afraid to use the media to get attention—through advertising or publicity. And she has always been willing to spend the time it takes to increase her visibility.

Sandi's first album came out with three others on Zondervan's Singspiration label—the Renaissance, "Moose" Smith, and Lillie Knauls—under a special promotion titled *Music Explosion.* In the December issue of *CCM* is a review of Sandi's first album, stating: "Word has been spreading for several months in Christian music industry circles that Sandi Patti was a singer to be on the lookout for. Well, this new album is proof that we have an extremely talented new singer on the scene." The review continues: "Sandi Patti sings like a bird. Her crystal-clear fluid voice interprets 'Precious Lord, Take My Hand'; it's Heaven time. There is an attempt to cover some contemporary material here . . . but Sandi's style is decidedly 'bright MOR,' and those types of songs work best."

The album, titled simply *Sandi's Songs,* was produced by Neal Joseph, an Anderson college graduate. It begins with "Jesus Is My Love Song to You." Published by Zondervan, the record company probably had some say in getting this song to Sandi. Most gospel record companies also have their own publishing companies and want artists to record as many company-published songs as possible. This increases the income for a label and, since so many first albums do not sell enough to make back the money invested, the extra income is sometimes a necessity.

"You're Such a Comfort to Me" is the next song on the album and is what is generally referred to as a "You" song. These songs refer to God or Jesus as "You" and not as God, Jesus, or Lord. The song can be interpreted, then, as a secular love song, but the true Christian knows that it's really about God. The unsuspecting listener, it is sometimes argued, hears this song and loves it and, when he finds out it is really about God, comes to a new appreciation of God and gospel music. It is an extension of the concept of the "personal" God and Savior who is a true love no less real than a boyfriend or girlfriend. These "You" songs were very popular in contemporary Christian music in the late 1970s and very early 1980s and went hand in hand with gospel's infatuation with pop music. The belief was that gospel's growth would come from the pop world of nonbelievers who would somehow hear gospel and decide it was O.K. to buy it in large numbers. Unfortunately, too many of these "You" songs were mindless drivel and did not appeal to either pop or gospel fans.

"When I Need Him" and "Precious Lord Take My Hand" are joined together in a medley and Sandi was really in her element with the production that builds to a full, big finish and the long, high vocal note at the end. Sandi sounds comfortable singing this classic hymn—but at this time, the contemporary audience was reluctant to sing old songs—they had a new life, a new faith, and they wanted new songs to go with them. It was not until the mid-1980s that this audience developed a sense of heritage and appreciation for history with their faith and music.

"He'll Never Let You Down" has a funky black gospel feel with the "God is Santa Claus" type of theology so prevalent in contemporary Christian music. The underlying belief is that God always answers prayers and, for the true believer, the answer is always "yes." Further, God is always looking out for your best interests and is providing you with all the perks, incentives, and promotions the true Christian deserves in life. Sandi and David T. Clydesdale wrote this song, which redeems itself from trite lyrics with a jazzy, Big Band sound at the end.

"I Could Never Have Imagined" is a piano ballad that tells how Jesus took away the singer's hopelessness and opened up her eyes to a charming world. This, too, is a popular theme—how life was so wretched and miserable before the singer finds Jesus but how absolutely wonderful and marvelous it is in the post-conversion stage. Listening to songs like this, one wonders what kind of lives these poor souls had to endure before their born-again experience. The simple answer is that most did not have to endure much hardship at all (except in the spiritual sense of wandering lost without a firm grip on the truth) and thus most of these kinds of songs lack depth.

Side Two begins with "You Never Gave Up on Me," written

by LaDonna Johnson, who is Larry Gatlin's sister. This song is a bright up-tempo number and is followed by a Phil Johnson song entitled "The Day He Wore My Crown." This was a hit for Johnson and later became a musical. The theme is atonement and again Sandi is beginning to find her element on this first album with songs like this, which are dramatic and picturesque.

"It's All Right Now" is written by Jessy Dixon and comes from the "things are real bad without Jesus, but boy are they great *with* Him" variety. Dixon did well with this song, which Sandi turns into a mellow up-tempo type ballad. "The Devil Is a Liar," a song from the group Seawind, is next and the Latin percussive feel probably seemed like a nice idea at the time but just doesn't seem to come off well.

The final song on the album is one Sandi wrote by herself, titled "Sandi's Song." Here, she uses her Karen Carpenter voice to say that her life is a song in a meandering montage of sentimentality and emotion. It is another "You" song and, though Sandi admits early in the song she is inarticulate, the listener keeps hoping for something more than the nebulous sentimentality that emerges. Still, there is an appeal here with her naïve sincerity.

This album could have been a Christian version of a Carpenters' album, still a strong influence on Sandi. But there were a few moments in the album when she showed the promise that would be fulfilled later when she had more confidence in herself and her material and knew where she fit in the contemporary Christian scheme.

14

The 1960s ended in outer space—with man successfully reaching the moon—but the 1970s were characterized by an attention to inner space, a searching for self-respect, a development of self-awareness, and a demand for self-image as the self emerged (often through psychobabble and mellowspeak) to dominate the decade and create a trend of national selfishness with very little counterbalancing self-control. Gospel music reflected this as more artists began seeing themselves as artists and musicians instead of ministers (the traditional self-image of gospel singers), while the gospel music industry began to promote itself earnestly and demand respect. It got it.

Those in the Christian culture saw and heard the gospel message become a big-time money-maker for the televangelists and witnessed a market network grow through the expansion of Christian bookstores permeating the land until Christianity became more than just a faith—it became a "target market," with demographics, psychographics, and its own vocabulary.

This vocabulary—or Christianese as it is sometimes called—gave new converts an immediate sense of belonging and self-identity with other believers as well as a sense of a "us versus them" mentality that invaded Christianity in the late 1970s and colored its relations and views of the secular world. Christians do not just talk, they "share," do not just socialize, they "fellowship," do not have drive and ambition, they have a "vision," do not speak of management in finances but of "stewardship," do not have professional or personal urges but a "calling," do not have a career but a "ministry," and are not just pleased or satisfied, they are "blessed." This common vocabulary gives a strength to a movement because it unites; the Christian culture of the late 1970s showed a unity that could not—and would not—remain through the 1980s, but it was a major factor in gospel music, making such a giant leap forward in the period from the late 1970s to the early 1980s.

For religion in general, there were movements and changes: The Eastern mysticism influence in the 1960s gave way to the cults of the 1970s. On one hand there was an incredible amount of religious acceptance as more religions sprang up, but as the Christian movement merged into the right-wing conservative movement of the early 1980s, there was less tolerance for those who believed anything other than fundamental Christianity. Still, the growth of the Christian culture and the rising fortunes of gospel music in particular owe a lot to their link with this conservative wave that was pushing toward the American shore at the end of 1979.

Perhaps the most significant event for the gospel music world in 1979 was the arrival of Bob Dylan's Christian album *Slow Train Coming.* The Christian music industry had long been infatuated with the pop world and the conversions of major celebrities and artists had always been seen as a major triumph and affirmation of the appeal of Christianity; perhaps the most prized catch of all was Bob Dylan. His conversion was expected to turn American pop music around. The theory was that someone of Dylan's magnitude—the "voice of a generation" who had the ears of almost every major rock artist, critic, and follower—would cause massive conversions from the rock 'n' roll world and the gospel fold would be multiplied mightily. Alas, it was not so.

Dylan's conversion caused more celebration in the gospel world than it did in the rock world, which regarded it primarily as an aberration and viewed it with alarm. Those who would follow whatever Dylan would say somehow could not bring themselves to follow him into this and the gospel world came face-to-face with a marketing reality: The future growth of gospel music would not come from acceptance by the secular—or nongospel—music world, but from better marketing within its own ranks. The infatuation with secular success and the strategies of marketing to the rock 'n' roll world gave way to the realization that gospel music's future was with the true believers and the key to big sales would be saturating the Christian marketplace through the Christian bookstores.

Gospel music is destined to be a minority in the music world because it cannot compete with rock on rock's terms. To do that would cause gospel music to lose its individuality and uniqueness. You cannot cross over from gospel unless you carry the cross over and the world of rock 'n' roll just doesn't want that kind of message hanging around. The gospel world, which toyed with the idea of watering down its message in a spate of "You" songs during the late 1970s, finally accepted its own audience. Thus, as Sandi Patti emerged in the early 1980s, the marketing system—and mentality—was coming into place for her to become a major act.

15

There was no Dove Awards show in 1979 because the Gospel Music Association had decided to shift the awards from the fall to the spring of the year, and since this transition would have meant a 1979 Dove Awards just a few months after the 1978 event, it was decided to skip 1979 altogether and hold the next one in 1980, seventeen months later.

The move to shift the Dove Awards was the major break with the Quartet Convention. The Southern gospel contingent had begun the GMA and the Doves had remained part of Quartet Convention Week activities, although the GMA had sought to include all facets of gospel music and convince the rest of the industry that it was not dominated by the Southern gospel faction. It was decided that the step to accomplish this was to hold the Dove Awards in the spring. The move worked and the Dove Awards increasingly became a showcase for contemporary Christian music in the 1980s as that segment of the gospel industry began to dominate the GMA and the awards, while the Southern gospel influence waned.

The 1980 Dove Awards were a disappointment in one area for the GMA: They had signed a contract with a Hollywood production firm to televise the event that year and expected this show to be their first national telecast. But the networks turned their thumbs down to gospel music—the market research people couldn't come up with enough "numbers" to placate executives nervous about the appeal of gospel—so the show's success had to be broadcast in the print media.

Sandi Patti's name was not on any of the nominations—there was no Artist of the Year award yet (the top award was for Male Gospel Group of the Year—a remnant from the Southern gospel heritage)—and those nominated in the Female Vocalist category were Cynthia Clawson, Vestel Goodman, Amy Grant, Evie Tornquist Karlsson, Janet Paschal, and Dottie Rambo. Cynthia Clawson won the award. The top song that year was "He's Alive" and the writer, Don Francisco, also captured the Songwriter of the Year honor. Bob Dylan won Gospel Album by a Secular Artist for *Slow Train Coming.*

The Grammy Awards featured lots of gospel music—there were performances by Andrae Crouch and the Mighty Clouds of Joy, as well as a tuxedo-clad Bob Dylan singing "Gotta Serve Somebody." Hosted by Andy Williams, the Grammy Awards featured five categories for gospel with B. J. Thomas, the Imperials, the Blackwood Brothers, and Andrae Crouch and the Mighty Clouds of Joy all carrying home an award, in addition to Bob Dylan, who won his first solo Grammy (he had previously been awarded a Grammy for being part of the *Concert for Bangladesh* album put together by George Harrison in the early 1970s) as Male Vocalist for his "Gotta Serve Somebody" single from the *Slow Train Coming* album.

In a *Billboard* article about the awards show, it was noted that "no less than seven times did Grammy recipients thank the Lord or God or Jesus for helping them achieve their coveted awards." This article cited the Barbra Streisand–Neil Diamond duet of "You Don't Bring Me Flowers" as the highlight of the show, but for those in the Christian community, the gospel message and gospel music on the Grammy telecast was the big news. For them, it meant a giant leap forward.

At this time, Sandi was singing in churches and at youth rallies, traveling about two or three weekends a month, and trying to put together longer tours that would last several weeks about four times a year. Setting up the sound and lights and running the control board that played Sandi's taped accompaniments, as well as booking the concerts was her husband John.

John loved the technical work and said at that time, "My experience comes mostly from the part-time work I was involved in at Anderson College. I worked on lighting for variety shows, musical concerts, and even dabbled in booking. This gave me experience in what it takes to put on a show and what is involved in a musical performance." In addition to handling the sound and lighting for his wife, John was in charge of lighting for the New York Summer Festival Series held at the Lincoln Center in New York during the summer of 1980.

Sandi loved having John travel with her and said, "I'm glad John travels with me as he does. I wouldn't be as comfortable doing this if he wasn't with me." Talking about her budding career during this time, she said, "It's hard for me to communicate thoughts verbally. I found that it was much easier for me to communicate through music. So I started doing more and more of it."

Sandi added, "I know how to sing and do all of the things a performer does, but without John managing my career, directing sound, lights, and handling all of my bookings, I could not do successfully all of the things that are expected of me."

Sandi's debut album had not generated much sales or created a great deal of excitement, but her appearance at the Christian Booksellers' Association Convention in July 1979 had brought her to the attention of a lot of industry executives.

Sandi had signed a contract for one album with Singspiration and when that contract was up, she and John began looking at other labels. They met with executives at Word and one executive who was involved in some of the meetings remembers: "John kept getting in the way—he was in way over his head with the talks and negotiations." Clearly, this shows the growing pains John and Sandi were going through as they were learning the ropes of the Christian music industry. John, particularly, had to overcome an overwhelming lack of experience and knowlege in Christian music circles as he sought to guide Sandi's career in these early stages.

Dan Johnson, another executive at Word, had been a music minister in Seattle before joining the record label and loved the kind of music Sandi was doing. Two major acts who appealed to church audiences—George Beverly Shea and the Bill Gaither Trio—had already been signed to Word and Dan wanted more artists like them. The signing of the Bill Gaither Trio (after more than ten years with the Benson Company) had surprised the industry and been a major coup for Word. But Sandi Patti would not be added to that roster—yet.

Sandi and John signed with the Benson Company because they felt the need for something different after working with Singspiration on the first album. Sandi said, "We looked at where Benson was heading, what advantages they had, and decided to go with them." They worked with Mike Cowart on the arrangements and negotiations and, as Sandi admitted at the time, "He's a big part of the reason we came with Benson."

The contract with the Benson Company was for one year and sessions for her album began in August 1980 in Nashville under the direction of producer Neal Joseph. The album was *Love Overflowing.*

Sandi was already showing characteristics that would distinguish her from most other Christian acts, spending a great deal of time and a lot of careful attention to the songs that would be on her records. She began looking for songs for the album in January. "We looked at well over a hundred songs before we chose the ten we wanted," she said. Sandi added, "Some of the songs I pick are those which work well in concert. But to me the lyrics are important. The music is purely secondary. If the words don't say anything, I won't do it. I usually read the lyrics before I'll even listen to it. The lyrics must be relevant, meaningful."

Talking about her future in 1980, Sandi was definitely indefinite. "I feel the Lord has taken care of me all my life. He has opened doors for me to travel, he opened a door for this new contract with Benson. I can only say that I have no plans for the future other than to continue like we are for now. As far as long-range plans, whatever is right will work out. When it's time to move on, the Lord will let me know it. I may be in this for life, or He may be letting me do this just for a short time."

Asked about the message she wanted to convey, Sandi answered, "Overall, I just want people leaving my concert feeling positive, feeling like 'Yes, God loves me!' That message is for everyone, from the grandmother who feels abandoned by her children to the tiniest child." She added, "I just want people to know that it's O.K. to serve the Lord. It's not an odd thing. You shouldn't feel bad or 'uncool' if you don't want to do drugs or drink. Christians can be the 'in' crowd, and should be. They should be the ones to set the example by which others want to strive to live."

She wanted audiences "to know that God is our friend. He's with us, on our side all of the time. You just have to have faith that He's working it out for us."

In early 1980 Sandi appeared in concert in Anderson with her parents. At this point, Ron and Carolyn Patty may have been considered bigger "stars" in gospel music than their daughter.

By this time, Ron and Carolyn Patty had had their own music ministry for a number of years, traveling to churches all over the country, as well as directing music for the Bill Glass Evangelistic Crusades. (Glass is a former pro football end.) Ron Patty also had a prison ministry, visiting fifteen to twenty prisons each year, where he held evangelical clinics for prisoners. Sports personalities such as Roger Staubach and Earl Campbell had joined him on these forays and Ron noted: "We usually see a fourth to a half of those inmates receive Christ into their lives. Many really are changed."

It was also during this time that Sandi made her first television appearances on "The PTL Club" and "The 700 Club."

16

The latest great wave of Christian revivalism began in the late 1960s. It was this revival that gave birth to contemporary Christian music. The Jesus Revolution reached young people caught up in the social/political turmoil that produced the civil rights movement, Vietnam, and Watergate within a ten-year period (1963–73). As a number of young people came to a Christian rebirth in their own lives, they saw the mainstream church as being unreceptive and irrelevant to their own culture. These young people had grown up on rock 'n' roll and music was important to them, so it was natural that they would use music as the great communication tool to spread their newfound faith.

The musical tone for the 1960s generation had been set in the 1950s. In 1955 Bill Haley and the Comets hit with "Rock Around the Clock," marking the official beginning of rock 'n' roll; in 1958 the Kingston Trio had a hit with "Tom Dooley," ushering in the folk movement. Both of these movements served as wedges for the generation gap: Rock 'n' roll freed the body, while folk music freed the mind. This led music into an activist period, as the rhythms of rock provided the soundtrack for teenage rebellion, while the lyrics of folk raised consciousness and pricked consciences.

Contemporary Christian music developed along the lines of pop and rock music throughout the sixties, seventies, and eighties, copying the sounds from pop radio and fitting Christian lyrics to them. But while rock fed on the rebellion inherent in the teenage years and directed it to a radical lifestyle *away* from the "norms" of societal expectations (to sex, drugs, booze, and so on), gospel rock led the rebellion toward a radical religion (a *living and personal* God).

The music of the 1980s has been guided by the three philosophies that have dominated the twentieth century in America: modernism, fundamentalism, and traditionalism. All three are connected to religion. Modernism (or liberalism) is a turning away from God toward science, humanism, and "art for art's sake." Fundamentalism is a radical interpretation of God as the dominant force in an individual's life and the Bible as God's Word speaking directly to man. Traditionalism is the blending of Christian principles and ideals with an increasingly technological and bureaucratic society. In music, avant-garde classical and rock represent modernism, gospel music comes from fundamentalism, while the main body of pop music is generally traditional. (Pop, as in "most popular," not necessarily defining a musical style.)

Mainstream Christianity, too, has been influenced by all three philosophies, simply because congregations are composed of people who live in the popular culture.

American Christianity has long been divided along racial lines —black and white—and gospel music roughly falls in these two distinct camps, too. In black gospel, there are two basic forms of music—a traditional sound composed primarily of large choirs and the rhythm and blues or "dance" sound, which is like the black music heard on the radio with gospel lyrics. The recordings reflect the taste of two different audiences with the choirs generally recorded live while the R&B sound comes from the studio.

In white gospel, there are three basic categories: Southern gospel, which is the sound akin to country music and dominated by male quartets; worship music, which is geared to be part of a church service; and contemporary Christian music, which is everything else. No matter what sounds there are in pop music—heavy metal, hard rock, country rock, easy-listening, jazz, new age, dance, acoustic, or anything else—there is a comparable sound in gospel music. This has led to the oft-repeated statement: "There is no such thing as gospel music—just gospel lyrics" because gospel (as in contemporary Christian music) virtually encompasses all forms, fads, and fashions in pop music.

Within contemporary Christian music there is a basic difference that comes from the attitudes of the audiences they reach. Some artists want to reach the "nonbeliever" or play music that is "evangelistic" with the intention of winning people to Christianity, while others direct their music to "the saints," or the Christian churchgoer who wants a music compatible with his beliefs.

There is also the issue of self-image in Christian music. What separates gospel from all other forms of music is that most of those involved in other forms of music see themselves as entertainers, while the gospel artist views himself as a minister. This leads to the endless debate that crops up among those who are interested and/or involved in Christian music. The essence of the debate is how pure ministry should be and whether gospel music is part of the show-biz industry or part of the church. The answers are different for each artist but, overall, the Christian artist must align himself with the church and his music must be viewed as part of an overall ministry to spread the gospel to either believers or nonbelievers.

17

The year 1980 ended on a sad note for those in the music world; John Lennon was shot down outside his apartment building in New York a couple of weeks before Christmas. For many, the prevailing mood was that an era had ended, an era that began on a Sunday night in February 1964 when the Beatles first appeared on "The Ed Sullivan Show." But as this era was closed, another era was just beginning: the era of the Reagan Revolution.

The Reagan Revolution officially arrived on January 20, 1981, when Ronald Reagan was sworn in as the fortieth President of the United States. His election meant a great deal to the Christian culture because, to a large degree, their votes had elected him; too, the conservatism inherent in mainstream Christianity now had a spokesman in Washington at the seat of power. The Reagan Revolution brought religion and politics together and this had an immediate impact on politics (the "born-again" experience became a litmus test for candidates), social issues (such as abortion and school prayer), culture (it was a badge of honor to be considered "Christian" and a mark of disrepute to be labeled "liberal"), and religion (which began getting major news coverage on a regular basis).

The evangelical community had been disappointed with Jimmy Carter. First, his politics (and the politics of the Democratic party in general) were a little too liberal to suit their tastes; too, they felt he had let them down on issues such as school prayer, abortion, and defense. When Ronald Reagan stepped in, saying the right things in the right language, the evangelical vote quickly switched. The fact his conservative politics was basically the same as theirs assured the Republican party of a loyal following in the coming years.

Reagan had campaigned with the theme: "Government isn't the solution. Government is the problem." He held a Republican businessman's view of government: "Less is better, none is best." This fit perfectly with the evangelical right, who have an innate disrespect for institutions and generally feel a discomfort with the rules that govern them. The right, led by no less than the President himself, felt that government was not only too big and burdensome but that it was a moral evil infecting American society. And so they would set about changing it, cleansing it, purifying it, and molding it to their own image. It was a heady time, a time when a feeling of adventure filled the air, a time when God was receiving an open invitation to be a part of politics, government, society, and culture. And the ones doing the inviting were His best friends.

Many people in gospel music saw a battle raging between good and evil—the righteous and the ungodly—and saw themselves as part of the force that would cleanse this country and lead it down the path of righteousness. As musicians, they saw their position akin to the position of the musicians in Jehoshaphat's army from the Old Testament—as leaders who would go before the army in the battle.

The Christian culture was growing and the Christian music industry was reaping the benefits. This industry kept growing when the rest of the music industry felt a big recession in 1980 and 1981. Gospel claimed itself "recession-proof," reasoning that in times of trouble people looked to spiritual solace, which included buying gospel albums.

At the 1981 Grammys, a major gospel performance was featured—"The Lord's Prayer"—which had more major gospel entertainers onstage at one time than in any previous Grammy show. In addition to composers Dony McGuire and Reba Rambo, there were the Archers, Cynthia Clawson, Andrae Crouch, Walter and

Tramaine Hawkins, and B. J. Thomas, who all performed on the album of the same title. This performance received one of the few standing ovations that evening. That album also won a Grammy for Best Gospel Performance, Contemporary or Inspirational.

The National Academy of Recording Arts and Sciences, composed primarily of people from the pop side of the music industry, had always tended to nominate and vote for gospel acts on major secular labels or acts who were most well-known to the secular world either because they had been around for so long (such as the Blackwood Brothers) or because they had been secular stars before going gospel (such as B. J. Thomas). But the 1981 gospel Grammy nominations were dominated by all-Christian labels, who captured seventeen of the twenty-seven nominations in the gospel categories.

The Reagan Revolution, which brought a number of evangelical Christians into the voting booths and got them involved in politics, had a direct influence on all this because people in the gospel music industry, inspired and influenced by the notion of activist voting, began to join NARAS in larger numbers. This represented a major change in attitude within the Christian community. Prior to this, evangelical Christians had shunned politics—many not even registering to vote—because it was considered a "worldly" pursuit, having nothing to do with their faith and irrelevant to their salvation. A similar view was held in gospel music concerning secular awards. Until 1980, a very large number of evangelical Christians did not bother to join the National Academy of Recording Arts and Sciences because they felt it was irrelevant to their mission: to spread the gospel through music. That attitude changed dramatically in 1980 and the results were the election of Ronald Reagan for President and a much greater involvement from Christian labels and artists in the 1981 Grammy Awards.

There were five categories for gospel music at the 1981 Grammy Awards. In addition to the album *The Lord's Prayer,* other Grammy winners were Shirley Caesar, the Blackwood Brothers, James Cleveland, and Debby Boone. Rev. James Cleveland and James Blackwood served as presenters during the evening, while the show's host, Paul Simon, noted: "For years gospel music has been divided into two categories—inspirational and contemporary—which is essentially a euphemism for black gospel and white gospel music." After a brief pause for heavy applause, Simon continued, "Of course, it seems God doesn't make the same distinction."

The biggest winner at the 1981 Grammys was Christopher Cross, who carried home five awards. His producer, Michael Omartian, is a Christian artist and was nominated in one of the gospel categories for an album he had done with his wife Stormie; thus, even the top winner in the pop categories had a gospel connection at this Grammy function.

The Dove Awards came in for some criticism this year. Among the musicians and singers involved in the contemporary Christian movement who had come out of the Jesus Revolution, there had always been a backlash against awards. The prevailing theme was that all rewards should be "heavenly" and that, somehow, giving awards to Christians from Christians for Christian endeavors was "ungodly." An editorial in the April 1981 issue of *CCM* titled "The Doves: What Kind of Strange Birds Are They?" by Karen Marie Platt reflected some of this attitude: "Anyone who loiters in the hall during and after GMA Week hears and overhears tremulous complaints and whispered dissent among the GMA flock. Humble magpies express discomfort with dispensing achievement awards for doing God's work. Lone eagles worry about the spiritual price of high-visibility expansion and mass approvals."

But after all this spiritual preening and proverbial gnashing of teeth about awards in general and Christian ones in particular, no one refused a nomination or an award. The participants who won all thanked God for giving His approval to their efforts.

Cynthia Clawson was named Female Vocalist for the second year in a row, Gary Chapman won Songwriter of the Year, Russ Taff won Male Vocalist, and album awards were won by the Hemphills, Larnelle Harris, Shirley Caesar, Teddy Huffam and the Gems, the Bill Gaither Trio, Debby Boone, and the ten artists on *The Lord's Prayer.*

The biggest winners that evening were the Imperials, who won three Doves, including the one for the newly instituted Artist of the Year award. This award was created to replace the Associates Award and gave the Doves one major overall award for the event. The GMA has two categories of membership—professional (those who work and receive income from gospel music) and the associates (or fans). The associates were only allowed to vote on one award, which until 1981 was the Associates Award and could be given to a person, group, song, or album. But from 1981 on, this group has been allowed to vote (with the professional group) on the Artist of the Year honor, so this award reflects the artist who appeals to professionals, amateurs, and fans in the gospel music industry.

The year 1981 was a landmark one for American Christianity in general and gospel music in particular. Two major record labels —CBS and MCA—began gospel divisions, Bob Dylan released his third gospel-influenced album *(Shot of Love),* and former top pop acts Al Green, Richie Furay, Maria Muldaur, and Bonnie Bramlett released gospel albums. On television, Barbara Mandrell featured a special segment on gospel (with contemporary Christian artists) on her weekly NBC show.

Christian labels were busy announcing that they had signed agreements with major secular labels for distribution, while Word, the label that dominates Christian music, celebrated its thirtieth birthday and began a video division. The Imperials were the major group in contemporary Christian Music, gospel artist Andrae Crouch released an album on Warner Bros., Amy Grant and Gary Chapman announced their engagement, and the contemporary Christian world received another gold album. *The Music Machine* by Candle was a revolutionary album because it showed the Christian market the tremendous appeal of children's music to the Christian culture, which is filled with young born-again parents wanting to raise their children on the gospel message. An onslaught of children's albums on Christian labels would follow in the 1980s.

In the world-at-large, there would be two attempts to assassinate world leaders in 1981—Pope John Paul II survived his wound, Egyptian President Anwar Sadat did not. In other news, 1981 was the year of the royal marriage—Prince Charles and Lady Diana—and the Rubik's Cube. Sandra Day O'Connor became the first woman Supreme Court judge, Lech Walesa received international attention leading striking workers in Poland, Bear Bryant became the winningest football coach ever, and Fernando Valenzuela was a rookie pheenom for the Los Angeles Dodgers.

18

Sandi Patti's "big break" occurred in 1981 when she became part of the Bill Gaither Trio spring tour and had a featured spot on the program. During the spotlighted segment, she sang "We Shall Behold Him," and the song and the artist both came to the forefront of gospel music. This was also the year *Love Overflowing* was released, which put her on the *CCM* charts with a single and album, both made popular by the tour.

Bill Gaither had known about Sandi for a long time. She often sang at Pinebrook, the studio he owns, and he knew her parents from college days in the 1950s. Gaither, always willing and eager to further young talent, wanted to help Sandi, but the timing had to be right. After she signed the Benson contract, he called and asked if she would like to join his touring show, singing backup as well as some featured solos. Sandi answered with an overwhelming yes.

Bill Gaither grew up in Anderson and attended Anderson College, graduating in 1959. While in college, he met Gloria Sickle and married her after her graduation in 1963. The couple then began teaching at Alexandria High School. He taught English and she taught French.

As a child, Bill learned how to play piano and organ and performed whenever he could throughout his school years, either in recitals or as an accompanist. After his college graduation, Bill taught high school for seven years, acquiring a master's degree in music at Ball State in Muncie along the way.

Gaither, along with his brother Danny and sister Mary Ann, began performing as the Gaither Trio in the mid-1950s, playing for civic clubs, Farm Bureau meetings, and in churches. In the early 1960s, Mary Ann left to get married and was replaced by Gloria. That move was the key to the success of the Gaithers, according to Bill, because it kept the group a family unit and because Gloria has a unique ability to "communicate" during her spoken monologues in songs and in the stories she tells during concerts.

The first album the Gaithers released for the Benson Company (they had previously recorded some custom albums) sold over 300,000 units—an unheard-of figure in gospel circles. The albums that followed also sold in six figures and quickly established the Gaithers as *the* major act in gospel music. Their success was built on their songwriting talents and they wrote such classics as "He Touched Me," "Because He Lives," "The King Is Coming," "Jesus, There's Something About That Name," and, later, songs such as "I Am a Promise," "I Am Loved," and "It Is Finished."

Bill Gaither made a very smart business move when he began songwriting: He formed his own publishing company and kept control of his own copyrights. His publishing company, begun in 1961, is the basis for his whole business operation, which grew to include ten Christian-related companies, including Pinebrook Studio, Spring House (a concert promotion and booking agency), Alexandria House (the largest source of sacred printed music in the country), Crystal Cathedral Choral Music Library (a number of anthems and choral collections distributed by Alexandria House), Ariose Music (a song publishing company), Printer Zink (a printing operation), the Gaither Music Company (for songs written by him and Gloria), Songbird, Inc. (which leases small planes), and Stage II Productions, which provides sound, lights, stages, and coaches for concerts.

Gaither has long been active in the affairs of Anderson College. He received an honorary doctorate in 1973 and in the spring of 1979 a building on the Anderson campus was named after him. The building, part of the $4-million Krannert Fine Arts Center, is the northernmost of the five units in the complex and has classrooms, music practice rooms, and instrumental and choral rehearsal halls. The dedication was held on April 26, 1979, and was highlighted by a visit from Charles Schulz, creator of Charlie Brown and Snoopy. Schulz had provided the funds for one of the buildings in honor of a longtime friend.

As the Gaither Trio wrote, recorded, and performed during those early days, each member continued to teach high school until 1967, when they began to devote all of their energies to gospel music. In the mid-1970s Danny left the trio for a career of his own and was replaced by Gary McSpadden as lead singer. The group was the first major concert draw in gospel music, appearing in civic centers and other venues outside churches. They were never a warmup for an evangelist (like many well-known gospel singers in the past had been) but established their reputation by performing in their own concerts.

Gaither admits, "The reason we began touring in the first place was that the ideas were bigger than the songs themselves." He also admits that there is a practical reason for touring that goes hand in hand with his songwriting. "When we're touring with a new song on the road, it allows us to see the reactions of people. We can get them involved singing and introduce each tune the way it was meant to be. I can't stress enough the importance of sharing music in a personal way with people, and allowing them to give you insights on your work."

During the period from 1979 to 1981, the Bill Gaither Trio was performing about 175 concerts a year, mostly on the weekends. It was a massive undertaking because at least nineteen people traveled with the show. Most of the musicians and crew traveled in a $170,000 custom-designed bus that allowed them to sleep as it drove through the night, while Bill, Gloria, and the female singers usually flew to the concerts in a leased private jet. Gary McSpadden, who was still pastoring a church in Fort Worth, Texas, at the time, generally arrived via commercial airline for the concerts.

After a Saturday night concert, Bill and Gloria would usually fly back home to take their kids to church on Sunday, while McSpadden would arrive in time to sing at his church and deliver a sermon.

Bill Gaither's favorite word is "communication" and he uses it often. For him, songwriting is a form of communication. "Music is a very usable item to me," he states. "It's just something I use to put my ideas in so I can get other people to listen to them." His concerts have always been efforts to translate his own Christian faith in a practical way so other people can live it too. "We're doing what we're doing because of what we believe," he has said. "We want to take a theological concept and make it work on Monday morning."

A Bill Gaither concert is like spending an evening with the Gaithers in their living room—at least that's the feeling Gaither tries to get across and usually does. Gloria is particularly adept at telling little stories with a slight break in her voice that pulls the emotional heartstrings in the audience. Bill tells stories too—about his life, about the songs, about his faith—and usually interjects a sense of humor into the program (although many accuse him of having an overabundance of corny jokes).

The songs hold the program together—and many in the audience know most of the songs the Gaithers sing—while Gaither keeps the program moving with a variety of styles and by spotlighting singers. This is where Sandi Patti received her first major exposure. She would be called out of the lineup of background singers to do a solo.

Bill Gaither's position as a cornerstone in contemporary gospel music is built on his songwriting and his constant preaching that it is the "message" in the song that is most important. Gaither's songs manage to embody everyday Christianity in a way that is theologically correct by American Christian standards, as well as entertaining, dramatic, perceptive, and enlightening.

Gospel is a lyric-dominated music. What is said in gospel is as important as *how* it is said. Furthermore, musical style must never take precedence over substance. Yet, for songwriting in general, the music is more important than the words. (A quick test will prove this: How many songs can you hum whose words you do not know? And how many times have you heard a melody and identified the song but are unable to name the song by words alone?)

The music is the most important element because it sets the mood and will be remembered most easily. The primary requirement of the lyrics, in this context, is that they do not clash with the melody—by either presenting an opposite emotion from the music, being filled with clichés or bad poetry, or by containing syllables that do not fit the rhythm and flow. Lyrics most "fit" the song in terms of rhyme, cadence, tone, syllables, and overall mood.

Bill Gaither is primarily the composer when he teams with his wife Gloria and she is primarily the lyricist. Often, the melody comes after the lyrics are written in the form of a poem or after the message has been decided upon. The genius of Bill Gaither is that he is able to compose memorable melodies *from* lyrics, making the lyric the centerpiece. He builds a music that delivers the message as powerfully as the words themselves. Too, his melodies are easily sung and remembered. They are accessible to most singers, and fit perfectly with congregations who can easily grasp the song and sing it from their church pews.

The mood Gaither usually creates is one that fits within a church sanctuary, powerful enough to move emotions, gentle enough to make a church audience comfortable, and memorable enough for people to remember it. Through this ability, Bill Gaither has emerged as the most important gospel songwriter and the most important figure in gospel music in the latter half of the twentieth century. And because he has done so with tremendous business sense, he has managed to build a miniempire in Alexandria, Indiana.

When Sandi began touring with the Gaithers, she knew how to sing but sensed a need for some dialogue to tie the songs together and put the concert in a perspective. She learned by studying Gloria

Gaither, who shared insights about herself, bantered easily with the audience, and created a warmth and closeness with the crowd in a concert setting. Gloria told Sandi that this ability would come in time. And in time, it did come.

19

Sandi's *Love Overflowing* album was released in March 1981 with a push from the record company, which had cranked up its publicity and marketing departments for her. Many Christian periodicals depend upon publicists with Christian companies to give them articles to run (they generally do not pay free-lancers). Record companies, knowing this, regularly supply articles from their publicity departments for these magazines. There were a number of articles on Sandi written by Cynthia Spencer, then a publicist for Benson. In addition, various radio and print ads were run, announcing Sandi's album along with the Gaithers' tour schedule.

The first single, "Down in My Heart," was released to eighteen hundred radio stations just before the album was shipped and a follow-up single was scheduled for three months later.

Singles were a hot issue at the time of *Love Overflowing*'s release. Secular record labels had long sent out 45s before an album—in some cases not even releasing an album until or unless a single was a hit. But gospel radio was used to getting an entire album and programming whatever cuts it felt appropriate for its audience. Since gospel radio viewed itself as a ministry, the programmers felt they should be allowed to choose the cut on an album they would like to program according to "God's will." The record companies, wanting to sell albums, knew that the success of a song (and album) depends upon people hearing it over and over. As it was, ten different radio stations could program ten different songs and, if a listener heard a song he liked, there was no guarantee he would hear it again anytime soon.

So Christian companies began to send out singles to focus attention on a particular song. Radio stations either had to play the single or refuse to air the act until the album came along. Since the single airplay charts were coming into their own, the success of a song could be quickly measured and since Americans are known for having national tastes, the success of a song in one market means it will probably be successful in other markets. The labels, knowing that radio stations often look to the charts to help make their decisions about which records to program, knew that if they could get a song on the charts, the chances would be much better that radio stations would play it and thus create a hit.

Sandi's first Benson album came in the midst of this controversy. No doubt, many radio programmers probably rejected the earlier single out of principle. Too, Christian radio demands that they "know" an artist before they will put them on the airwaves, and Sandi just wasn't known well enough yet.

Another issue with gospel radio concerned the National Religious Broadcasters (NRB), the chief spokesman and lobbying arm for gospel radio programmers since its inception in the early 1940s.

For years, the NRB had represented the "preaching and teaching" programs, the nonprofit stations, and the programs headed by a preacher whose main thrust was "spreading the Gospel." But as contemporary Christian music came along, and young listeners wanted radio to play *music* rather than preach, the NRB looked dangerously out of step.

Sandi performed at a "miniconcert" one afternoon at the NRB's 1981 convention. It was in a small room, with some 150–200 radio programmers drifting in and out. It was a small step for the NRB powers to come to grips with the musical wave descending upon them. The future years saw the NRB increasingly accept contemporary Christian music, but that first audience must have been tough for Sandi because most of the people listening thought that music should be an audience's preliminary to a sermon.

Sandi first reached the *CCM* charts in the inspirational/MOR category with her song "We Shall Behold Him" in the August/September issue. It entered the charts at number thirteen.

The first single from the album had failed to attract any significant airplay and therefore the album went unnoticed. The second single selected was "Home of the Lord," a duet with Russ Taff, who was still with the Imperials and who had been teamed with Sandi to help give her some credibility and visibility with radio programmers. But it was the B-side of that single, "We Shall Behold Him," which became the hit. The reason: She was performing it in every one of her concerts with the Bill Gaither Trio. The record label had put this song on the B-side of her second single, but had serious doubts about whether this was a radio song or was instead geared exclusively to the live concert setting.

In the success of "We Shall Behold Him" is another insight to the success of Sandi Patti—she seeks to record songs that can be performed live to a church audience rather than songs which can only work in a studio or on radio. Since she knows her audience so well, she has an innate sense of which songs will appeal.

There was a huge recession in the country at the time of the Christian Booksellers' Convention in 1981, but sales for Christian music were up from the previous years. This caused the Christian industry to again brag a bit about being "recession-proof" and offer as an explanation that "people turn to the Gospel in troubled times." The truth of the matter, however, probably rested in the fact that Christian bookstores were finally accepting Christian prerecorded music product as a legitimate part of their inventory.

There had always been a bit of conflict between books and music with retailers, and their name "Christian booksellers" indicates which side most stores chose to take. However, with sales of music accounting for 17 to 40 percent of a stores' revenue, the owners quickly saw they must get more heavily involved in stocking music. Too, the growth in the Christian culture meant more

Christian consumers. It also meant more Christian bookstores, which meant more sales of Christian albums.

Finally, the early reluctance of Christian bookstores to stock contemporary Christian music was fading. The store owners had looked on early gospel rock as music from the Devil, unsuitable for their stores, and some customers—mostly older ones—had complained about rock 'n' gospel. However, as contemporary Christian music grew and people began to see it as a wholesome alternative to real rock 'n' roll for their own children—some of the barriers began to fall away.

Thus, the recession of 1981 did not hit the Christian record companies because stores and consumers were playing "catch-up" with the product. Its sales success was a matter of filling a void already created in the marketplace, providing a supply for a demand already there.

In October "We Shall Behold Him" moved up to number eight on the airplay charts and *CCM* gave a review to five albums entitled "Five Ladies in Waiting." It states, "[In Christian music] women, especially, have been robbed of the right to uniqueness. Female vocalists have been told to stand still, smile wide, be sure to wear pink and look 'sweet.' Unfortunately, in today's plastic society, that which is sweet often turns out to be saccharin, or simply have no substance at all—just lots of empty energy."

This reviewer then went on to state, "For the most part, what we have . . . is the sugar blues." The reviewer concludes, "Now don't get us wrong. We love our sisters in Christ . . . We would just like to get to know them each and every one . . . at a time, please."

Actually, the *Love Overflowing* album—except for "We Shall Behold Him"—does not really stand out from the other four albums released at that time. Sandi had not quite found her niche and did not have the budget for experimentation or the kind of orchestration that showcases her talents best.

The first cut on the album is "Down in My Heart," which

Sandi wrote with Gary Chapman. (Sandi had a major hand in the music, but not the lyrics.) It is a bright up-tempo song of Christian escapism (no pain with Jesus) and this "You" song probably became the label's first choice for a single because it presented the bright and rosy picture of Christianity so appealing to that culture.

The song "Love Overflowing," like many other contemporary Christian songs, could serve as an advertisement for Jesus, offering a growing joy and a new deal better than anything else before or since. "So Far" could have been a Karen Carpenter song with the "You" lyrics, although the concepts of "fight" and "battle" in the Christian life are introduced and, although the warrior/God does not appear in this song, the concept is there.

Side Two begins with the most cooking song on the album. "The Home of the Lord" is a duet with Russ Taff and Russ's gritty vocals and the meaty lyrics give this a solid feeling different from the wishy-washy emotionalism of some of the other numbers. "Somebody Believed" sends the message that faith can overcome even the seemingly impossible and biblical examples back up this claim.

The fourth song on Side Two is "We Shall Behold Him" and, in hindsight, this is an odd place for this song. Many producers and artists quietly concede that when they want to bury a weak song, it is usually Side Two, cut four. But on this album, the *strongest* song is placed here. Perhaps this, of all the songs, did not quite "fit" the concept of a contemporary Christian album at the time and, though Sandi was doing the song in her live performances, it somehow clashed with the rest of the material.

It is difficult—if not impossible—to determine why a certain song is a hit and another is not. But looking at "We Shall Behold Him," some things stand out. First, writer Dottie Rambo used the word "behold" to capture the moment of seeing God. Although "see" or "look" mean essentially the same thing, there is a power and majesty in "behold" that says this meeting is momentous. The picturesque lyrics that present applauding stars, thunder, light, and an unfolding sky give a poetic drama that the Christian audience finds particularly appealing. And, of course, the soaring melody that captures this grand drama as it unfolds delivers an entire pageant. Too, the Christian lives for his heavenly reward and this song assures him of it. Mark Twain once observed a man "with the calm self-assurance of a Christian with four aces" and this same self-assurance is what true believers possess regarding their salvation and heavenly reward. To have that articulated in such stirring poetry is a reward in itself.

Sandi's voice, which begins the song a cappella, and the production, which builds to a huge ending, convey the message perfectly and provide the drama the song demands. Like a number of other major artists from all music fields, Sandi found her true identity and niche when she found the hit song that would separate her from the rest of the pack in contemporary Christian music.

Love Overflowing first reached the *CCM* album charts in the December 1981 issue of the magazine, coming on at number forty-three. However, it was not listed by any of the magazine staffers or critics as a favorite in the "Editor's Choice" section in the same issue of the magazine.

Meanwhile, back in Anderson, Indiana, Sandi's parents, Ron and Carolyn, had their turn in the spotlight. At the Anderson College homecoming the Christian Brothers Quartet reunited for two concerts. Joining Ron and Carolyn were quartet members Doug Oldham, Ernie Gross, Jr., and Paul Hart. The concert was dedicated to former member Paul Clausen, who had been bedridden for a number of years with Huntington's disease.

For Sandi, 1981 was a big year for personal appearances as audiences began to hear from her. She played 175–80 dates this year—about 75 percent in churches—including the concerts with the Gaithers. She also opened for B. J. Thomas in Nashville, performed at the Christian Booksellers' Association of Canada's meeting, and made her first appearance at the Christian Artists Seminar in Estes Park, Colorado.

Sandi also performed at the Gaithers' Praise Gathering in Indianapolis, and on New Year's Eve in Hollywood, where Pat and Shirley Boone received the Christian Achievement Award from the World Wide Pictures and Jubilate organization.

20

The gospel music industry formally recognized Sandi Patti in 1982 when she was nominated for two Dove Awards. Sandi was nominated for Female Vocalist and Artist of the Year, while the song "We Shall Behold Him" was one of the ten nominees for Song of the Year. Ironically, Sandi's album was *not* nominated in any category: She was known for singing a great song, but not as an album artist or as a major concert draw of her own.

The Doves were the highlight of Gospel Music Week. It would be a big night for Sandi and she knew it—the whole family gathered in Anderson for the drive down.

Sandi did not have to wait long in the show for her first award. Doug and Laura Lee Oldham—old friends of the Patty family—presented her the Dove for Female Vocalist. She was competing with Cynthia Clawson, Tanya Goodman, Amy Grant, Reba Rambo Gardner, and Christine Wyrtzen.

Accepting her first award, Sandi said, "I am so thankful to be associated with such a fine bunch of musicians who have so much more a purpose for singing than just the joy of music."

Later in the evening, Sandi performed three songs nominated for Song of the Year: "Soldiers of the Light" by David Baroni, "Trumpet of Jesus" by Michael and Stormie Omartian, and "We Shall Behold Him," which won Song of the Year for writer Dottie Rambo. The audience—comprised of many who were hearing her for the first time—gave Sandi a tremendous standing ovation when she was finished.

Competing for Artist of the Year honors were Cynthia Clawson, Andrae Crouch, Dallas Holm, Sandi, and the previous year's winners, the Imperials. It was quite a surprise—even for Sandi—when she won the award because Sandi was the dark-horse candidate, since the other artists were more established in the gospel world and already had successful careers. Sandi had only two albums out—neither of which was particularly successful (in fact, the first album was all but forgotten)—and her career at this point was tied strongly to the Gaithers' tours and to "We Shall Behold Him." But those connections and performances paid off. Gospel music was ready for some "new blood" who appealed to the church audience. Enter one Sandi Patti.

At the Grammys a week before, Sandi had not even been nominated; this audience was still unaware of her. Still, the Grammys made another step forward with gospel music by featuring lively performances by several entertainers. Christian record labels showed a real surge in voting strength as they captured twenty-two of the twenty-eight nominations in the gospel categories.

"Gospel" was a real buzzword on this Grammy night, hosted by John Denver. Numerous acts thanked the Lord or expressed an interest in recording gospel albums in the future. Among these were the Pointer Sisters, Ben Vereen, the Oak Ridge Boys, and James Brown.

However, there were several prevailing attitudes in the Christian music industry about pop music's interest in gospel at this time: (1) gospel music should only be recorded by Christians; (2) the Christian music industry decides or "knows" which singers/artists are really "Christians"; and (3) gospel music must have a life-changing effect on people listening to it or it is not really gospel music. Although they tried not to admit it, Christian artists were jealous of the secular success of pop acts who recorded gospel songs because the gospel artists felt this was *their* terrain.

In 1982—especially after the Doves—Sandi began receiving

press coverage beyond what Benson generated. The first major story before the Doves was in January in *CCM,* which said, "Sandi sees her ministry as that of encouragement, and edification to the body. She realizes that most people who come to hear her are church people, college age and up. She does not try to evangelize, nor to overspiritualize. She wants to share Jesus in the most loving fashion she knows—she sings."

Sandi said, "I feel that music is the best way to communicate what one is feeling inside . . . I try to bring a real positivenesss to my messages and the songs that I sing, so that maybe the people can leave the concert feeling very uplifted and positive about the Christian way of life, and know that Jesus loves them."

In an interview with *Christian Review* after the Dove Awards, Sandi said, "I often have a hard time expressing myself when meeting new people, but I have felt that music is an outlet for me. It helps me to express emotions that I have a hard time expressing otherwise." She also reaffirmed her commitment to singing gospel music. "I think all music is very special and I like it all, but I feel like I would be wasting a gift from the Lord if I were involved in music only for pure enjoyment. There has to be something more meaningful, something more than just enjoyment. I want to sing about the Lord."

Already, Sandi was beginning to see the privileges afforded a singer. "Through using music, you can get the attention of some that you might not otherwise get," she said. "You can share with them through the words of a song or through things that are said during a concert. I enjoy sharing about my life, my husband, and what the Lord has done for us. Music opens a lot of doors."

She was also learning about audiences. "I've realized that you can't fool [them] . . . but they will be very receptive to someone who they sense has a genuine and honest heart. You can't go up there trying to pull one over on them or they'll just turn you off." Asked about her future, she said, "I feel like I will probably always be involved in music in one way or another. I have a real burden for music education or to work in music therapy. Music goes through walls that other things can't. I feel that for some people with emotional and mental problems music has been a redeeming factor. So I probably will not be doing concerts all my life, but I think I will always be involved with music. On a one-to-one basis, I want to help heal people's emotional hurts and spiritual hurts through music."

Later that spring, Sandi's album *Lift Up the Lord* came out and this time around *CCM* gave it a strong, positive review. Written by editor John Styll, the review began, "Look out world, here comes Sandi Patti! She recently took home Dove Awards for Gospel Artist of the Year and Female Vocalist . . . and when you hear this album you'll know why. She's easily one of the most talented singers to come along in a long while."

Perhaps another early review points out a reason for the success of *Lift Up the Lord.* It said, "Most 'praise albums' make great background music for senior citizens' potlucks, but not this one!" It went on to point out the joy and power in the upbeat album. A flier sent to sales and promotion personnel at Benson said, "The material on this album provides more of what so many people stood up and applauded when Sandi Patti sang on tour with the Bill Gaither Trio . . . Greg Nelson has produced an album that allows Sandi to showcase her talent, yet control it enough to accomplish the purpose of communication of the message of Jesus Christ, not focus all the attention on her talent."

This in-house flier further notes that it is not just her talent as a singer but her message and the way she communicates it that makes her so appealing to audiences. This flier also notes that she had been performing on tour with the Bill Gaither Trio, "giving her exposure to more people than many performing artists get in their entire careers." The album was chosen Album of the Month by Benson, which means that the sales, marketing, and promotion people made it their top priority. Their efforts soon paid big dividends.

The album is unabashedly and unashamedly Christian; more than that, it is a "praise album" meant to be heard and sung in the context of God as an audience. The feeling among many in the contemporary Christian culture is that God enjoys being praised, that He finds accolades, and songs sung to Him extolling Him to be pleasing; further, it is believed that the greatest gift we can give to God is our hearts or love and that we show this by a songful devotion to Him. It is another example of man communicating directly to God (worship), while God communicates directly to man (approval).

The first song on the album is "Lift Up the Lord," an up-tempo song with lots of horns and a "jazzy" feel. Sandi is one of the cowriters on this song (along with Billy Smiley and Gary McSpadden) and the publisher is listed as Sandi's Songs, the company she and John began for her copyrights. This is interesting because it shows more power and independence on her part with her new recording contract (on the previous albums, the songs she wrote were published by the label's publishing company). An increasing knowledge and awareness on the part of her and John is also displayed—there's money to be made in controlling the publishing rights.

The first hit single, "How Majestic Is Your Name," with its catchy piano riff, was written by Michael W. Smith with the lyrics taken directly from Psalm 8. A number of church congregations now sing this song, proving the appeal to this audience and the taste of Sandi Patti.

A Barbra Streisand-like ballad, "They Could Not," follows and the message is that "they" (who are never really identified—though the true believer *knows* who "they" are) could not understand Jesus when He walked the earth, and could not hold Him down when they put Him in the grave. It is a Resurrection song with a new twist to the old story.

Side One closes with a beautiful ballad, "Jesus, Lord to Me," which provides beautiful orchestration to deliver the message of this confessional prayer. This song fits perfectly in the church sanctuary—which is where Sandi's fans sit regularly—and there is even a section of a cappella, congregational-type singing to bring home the point that this isn't just a song, it's a church service too!

Perhaps the major change in this album from the previous two Sandi Patti albums is the addition of Greg Nelson on the team as producer. For the first time, Sandi was directed by someone with the singular vision and desire to reach the church audience with their kind of music. This audience wants a religious experience when they listen to an album, and this album provides that.

Greg Nelson was raised in a mainstream evangelical church in North Dakota. He attended the University of North Dakota, then went to the Institute of Biblical Studies in San Bernardino, California, where Campus Crusade has its school. Nelson met Michael Omartian there and together they played in a group called New Folk.

Nelson returned to North Dakota after these adventures and taught school for seven years, in addition to pursuing his interest in contemporary Christian music by putting together a studio in his basement where he recorded albums and commercials. Phill McHugh's first two albums came from this basement studio.

After teaching, Nelson became a youth counselor at his church and spent the next couple of years ministering to high school kids, playing in a music group, and—for a while—directing the Bismarck city orchestra. He began his own record label, Spirit Records, which started the careers of Benny Hester; Albrecht, Roley, Moore; and Ark. Soon he signed a distribution agreement with Sparrow Records that led to a relationship with label head Billy Ray Hearn. Nelson ended up in Los Angeles as director of publishing for Sparrow after selling his own label.

Moving to Nashville to do some arranging, Nelson's plans somehow fell through and he found himself sleeping on a friend's bedroom floor while his wife and daughter remained in Los Angeles. He made the rounds from gospel office to gospel office and finally landed work remixing some albums for Zondervan and producing an album by Wayne Watson. Then Ray Nenow—the friend who provided his bedroom floor to Greg—asked him to produce Joe English's *Light of the World* album and this project yielded two number one songs and was considered one of the top albums of

1981. After this, he produced albums for the Cruse Family, Pat Boone, Bonnie Bramlett, Cheryl Prewitt, the Richard Smallwood Singers, Gary McSpadden, and others.

After the first rush of success, Nelson came into demand as a producer and produced albums for Steve Green, Larnelle Harris, Connie Scott, Stephanie Boosahda, and Andrew Culverwell, in addition to Sandi. Along the way, he also wrote "Without You," "People Need the Lord," "All Over the World," and a number of others—usually with a cowriter.

Nelson is a stickler for great songs and states emphatically, "I . . . endeavor to find great material. I try to find songs which communicate to people—to the plumber, the waitress, and to the doctor or lawyer as well. The songs that hit a need everybody needs to hear." His role with Sandi is crucial. As her producer, Nelson emphasizes that he feels two major obligations: "One is to make sure the songs 'feel right' when they're recorded, and the other is to minister to the artist, to let them see how important the lyric is. It's a very tough thing to find great lyrics and great music together. It's twice as hard to find inspired lyrics anointed by the Holy Spirit."

Sandi, too, insists on great songs and states, "I've got about ten people constantly on the lookout for songs for me to listen to. I take the ones they suggest and read the lyrics first, before I ever hear the music. If the words say something I believe or want to say, then I listen to the music. If the two compliment each other, then you've got a really good song and I'm interested."

The teaming of Sandi with Greg Nelson was another critical step in Sandi's career. He came along at a time when Sandi needed a clear focus so that her career would take off. Greg Nelson played a key role in bringing all this together.

21

The Christian media discovered Sandi in a big way in 1982 and there were features, reviews, pictures, and column mentions in periodicals such as *CCM, Encore, Charisma, Windstorm, In Touch, Group, Rocking Chair, Christian Bookstore Journal, the Singing News,* and others. In addition to helping Sandi's career by making her more visible, it also helped the Christian culture get to know her better.

Early in the year, Sandi, along with the Bill Gaither Trio and Doug Oldham, were featured on a national telecast of "The Doctor Is In," a prime-time presentation by the Church of God in Anderson that also featured *Peanuts* cartoonist Charles Schulz and his own animated cartoons. This show was carried on a number of local TV stations. Later the Barn recording studio gave Sandi an Excellence of a Recorded Product Performance award, which was created especially for Sandi to honor her accomplishments.

At the end of the year, Sandi joined artists Jimmy Owens, Chris and Carole Beatty, Otis Skillings, Dino Kartsonakis, Larnelle Harris, the Hawaiians, Steve Camp, and Barry McGuire in Singapore for the first Christian Artists Seminar in Asia. Organized by Cam Floria, it followed the same format of seminars and concerts as the two he had previously organized in Estes Park, Colorado, and De Bron, Holland.

Sandi toured Australia as the opening act for the Imperials and was in Indianapolis again for the Gaithers' Praise Gathering. But she was learning the rigors of the road as well as the benefits. She told one reporter, "There are some people who look at me and say, 'This can't be real. This can't be the fun and games she makes it out to be.' I really don't try to project that picture. It is hard work. It drains you when you miss your plane connections, then you arrive at your destination but your luggage doesn't; you don't have anything appropriate to wear to the concert, but luckily you've carried your soundtracks with you so at least you've got an orchestra. These kinds of things aren't fun and games, but if something is worth doing, you go ahead and do it in spite of the obstacles. I only need to know that I am where God wants me to be and that I'm doing what He wants me to be doing."

Sandi needed to be well-adjusted to the traveling and hectic pace. After her big wins at the Dove Awards, she received eight hundred requests for personal appearances for the rest of 1982.

A concert in Anderson, Indiana, served as the unofficial kickoff for the *Lift Up the Lord* album, which had been released in March. It seemed to be the appropriate place for this event. "We couldn't think of anyplace we'd rather do it than here, before a hometown crowd," Sandi said. "People at the college have watched me grow up and they've always supported me and believed in me. Probably the most common comment I get from them now is 'See? I told you so.' "

After that concert, college president Robert Reardon came up to Sandi and reminded her, "We believed in you and loved you a long time ago. These record people are just jumping on the bandwagon. Remember, we started you out."

It was also during this time that Sandi and John, along with her parents, Ron and Carolyn, were honored as Distinguished Alumni at the Alumni Banquet at Anderson College. This banquet was held just before the college commencement in June, which kicked off the annual International Convention of the Church of God.

Sandi and John indulged in what she called their big splurge in their marriage—they bought a home. It is in the suburbs of Anderson and fits Sandi's self-image as a wife and homemaker. "I needed to be a housewife in a real neighborhood," she said. "When we're on the road there's something nice about knowing we have a home to go to where we can refuel and recharge our batteries. We're nothing special here."

At this time, Sandi was still having some second thoughts about spending so much of her life on the road. She said, "I guess you're always envious of whatever somebody else has . . . you know, the grass-is-always-greener syndrome. But there are times in my life when I would very much like to have dirty laundry to do and kids tugging at the hem of my skirt. People who hear me say that might think I'm crazy, but there's nothing like normalcy in your life, and I really don't have that right now. I love what I do, but every concert is different, every hotel room is different, everyone we meet on the road is different. Sometimes I get hungry for normal kinds of things that I can count on, whether it's kids around the house or the fact that my husband will walk in the door every night at five o'clock sharp."

Gradually, though, Sandi was learning to adjust to a hectic life. "I've begun to read my Bible on the plane. Rather than getting a magazine and filling my mind with recipes, I fill it up with Jesus talking to me. That kind of charges up my battery so I can have the energy it takes to do a concert, minister to people, and allow the Lord to work through me." She also admitted that it helped her in dealing with people she came into contact with after the concerts. "I can't go into a situation unprepared and expect that just because I've done it over and over, the same results are going to happen," she said. "It doesn't work that way. A lot of young people are listening to what I'm saying and I want to take advantage of that opportunity to share some life-changing things with them . . . Because of some good experiences and some very hard experiences that I've had . . . I think I have more to share now. It's a lot easier to talk when you have something to say. It gives you some meat."

With the sudden rush of success, Sandi tried to put her career in perspective. In an interview with Bob Darden for the Waco newspaper, she said, "I really wasn't planning to go into professional music at all. I'm still amazed at how it all came about . . . With *Love Overflowing,* it just seemed that all of the right ingredients came together. I was certainly fortunate to be one of the first people to record 'We Shall Behold Him.' At the time I was traveling with the Bill Gaither Trio, and that got me before a lot of people. So I guess the right exposure and the right song at the right time sort of accelerated the process. I don't know why God chose to work that way, but He did."

When asked in 1982 about her future, Sandi always admitted that she and John wanted to begin a family. "Somewhere down the road I'd love to be involved with handicapped or autistic children, especially in the areas of special education or music therapy." She was seeing things happen in her concerts that were moving her as much as they moved audiences. "I've seen so vividly the healing power of music," she said. "I've seen it break down so many walls."

Sandi also felt a strong bond with her audience during this time, as she worked out the relationship between performer and audience. "So many times I wonder, 'What do I have to offer someone in an hour and a half that is more special than an evening at home?' " she reflected. " 'What can I leave them that is worth the time they spend with me?' It's got to be more than just me standing on the stage and singing a bunch of songs. I want to bring a positive message to church people; I want to leave them with positive feelings about themselves. I know it sounds so simple and trite, but I want them to know that Jesus loves them. There are a lot of times that so many other things get said and we forget that there is someone who cares about us individually—through the good times and the bad. If I can communicate that to only one person in each concert, then I have succeeded."

About Christianity, she said, "One of the biggest lessons I'm learning right now can be summed up in one word: commitment. We as Christians need to have a commitment with God daily. It's not a one-time thing where you expect the rest to take care of itself.

It's got to be a renewed commitment. It's like going on a diet. You're committed, but if you don't think about it consciously every day, and recommit yourself, you're not going to be effective. It's the same with the Christian way of life, to be committed to the Lord in Bible study every day, prayer every day."

A change in perspective was seen from Sandi and John's professional view of themselves in 1982: They stopped calling their organization John Helvering Ministries and began calling it the Helvering Agency.

22

"We Shall Behold Him" remained in the top ten of the airplay charts until August and finally dropped off the charts in December. The *Love Overflowing* album was on and off the charts all year, generally in the forties, while *Lift Up the Lord,* which first appeared on the May chart, finished the year at number seven. "How Majestic Is Your Name," the single from the new album, had chart success on both the inspirational and adult contemporary charts and stayed in the top ten from June through December. But the charts at the end of 1982 were dominated by Amy Grant, whose *Age to Age* album entered at number one in July and remained there throughout the year. "Sing Your Praise to the Lord" and "El Shaddai" from that album dominated airplay in Christian radio. Still, Sandi was clearly mounting a challenge.

This was a solid year for Sandi, as significant sales were beginning with *Lift Up the Lord.* She had escaped the "sophomore jinx" with "How Majestic Is Your Name," which provided the perfect follow-up to "We Shall Behold Him." Both songs, while different in tempo and tone, reached the same audience—the church—as Sandi further established herself in that market.

The first singer to become a star to the church audience in the latter half of the twentieth century was George Beverly Shea. Shea achieved this through his appearances on network radio and as the soloist for Billy Graham. He is linked closely with the hymn "How

Great Thou Art," which he introduced to American audiences during Graham's Toronto Crusade in 1955. The song became a standard during the 1957 New York Crusade at Madison Square Garden, where Shea performed it ninety-nine times during the sixteen-week stay.

Shea differed from other singers who had achieved their fame as the singing partner of an evangelist (such as Ira Sankey with Dwight Moody and Homer Rodeheaver with Billy Sunday) because records, radio, and—later—television allowed him to have a separate identity from the evangelist. Shea's recordings on RCA, begun in 1951, sold well and firmly established him as the premier singer of hymns and other religious songs for the church audience in the 1950s and early 1960s.

Mahalia Jackson achieved fame as a gospel singer in the 1950s and 1960s, too, but she was known to those outside the gospel world who did not particularly care for gospel music but who loved her great talent. Too, her base of support was the black church and American Christianity has long been divided between black and white, with white Protestants generally keeping a distance from black Christianity (which many in the charismatic Christian group feel reluctant to accept as truly Christian), so white church audiences never really accepted her as one of their own.

The first star in contemporary Christian music was Evie Tornquist. A small, blond-haired, blue-eyed young lady from New Jersey, Evie is pert and pretty. Vocally, her style resembles Sandi's; her trained voice would fit nicely into a church choir. Evie was the darling of the gospel world both here and in Europe—where she was discovered—in the 1970s. Her album sales were well over the 100,000 mark for each release and many felt she would carry the banner of contemporary Christian music to the secular world in the mid-1970s when gospel music was struggling for recognition and acceptance.

Several gospel artists had tried for secular success and failed—the Oak Ridge Boys were the most visible examples in the early 1970s. They were at the top of the Southern gospel world—selling over 100,000 albums on each release—and playing to capacity crowds—when they decided to sign with CBS. They recorded gospel music for several years, but CBS could not sell the records and the Oaks saw their sales slip to nearly nothing during this transitional period. They switched labels and continued to sing gospel, but soon realized they could not get their gospel songs on country/pop radio or in the hands of consumers. So the Oaks began recording country music. Their immense talents again came to the forefront and they were soon recognized as the top group in country music, paving the way for acts such as Alabama and numerous others who have followed.

Evie did not sign with a secular label or stop singing gospel music. Instead, she got married and placed her husband Pele Karlsson and their new baby at the center of her life. She stopped recording and touring, devoting herself to being a wife and mother. When she did return to gospel, she directed her energies to the church. Pop success never really was a consideration for Evie; she and her husband definitely wanted a ministry and thus stayed within the gospel community.

B. J. Thomas had a celebrated conversion in the mid-1970s that took him away from drug addiction to a born-again experience. Thomas had been a pop star before his conversion (he had reportedly sold 32 million records with hits such as "Raindrops Keep Falling on My Head," "Somebody Done Somebody Wrong Song," and others) and afterward began recording Christian music for Word Records. He, too, was a bright star in the crossover arena, but soon developed problems with his concerts when two sets of fans showed up—one group wanting the old pop hits, the other wanting just gospel. Thomas tried to reconcile the two, singing all his old hits while closing with his testimony, but the conflict proved too much and he moved out of gospel again. Somehow the Christian audiences could not accept B. J. Thomas as a Christian entertainer. They wanted him all or nothing, so Thomas stopped recording Christian music on gospel labels and began recording country music.

Debby Boone had the biggest hit of 1977—"You Light Up My Life"—and was on her way to being the star who could bridge the gospel and secular world. She followed this with a number one song on the country music charts, but again a husband and family took precedence. She withdrew from her performing career to a more low-key life with occasional performances and records. Debby Boone was never really comfortable as a pop star—she is grounded too deeply in the Christian culture—and as her Christian records gained a wide acceptance, she realized she was more at home as a gospel artist. Still, she continued to perform in secular venues, such as Las Vegas, and continued receiving some attention from the secular media.

Cynthia Clawson emerged briefly in the late 1970s as Evie's star faded, but Clawson was not really comfortable with the church audience—she longed to record pop material—so her reign ended in 1980 after capturing two consecutive Doves for Female Vocalist. Cynthia began recording on Triangle, a small label that had trouble distributing her records adequately. She signed with CBS's gospel label Priority, begun in 1982, but fate was cruel again. When the top brass at CBS in New York shut down their gospel division in 1983—just as it was on the verge of becoming a major force—she was left with legal ties to a defunct label. Clawson certainly has the talent—her voice is perhaps even more impressive than Sandi's—but she never really put together an effective team for her career.

Amy Grant is quite another story. Beginning in the gospel field with her debut album in late 1976, she first established herself firmly with Christian audiences, giving her a base from which to work. The breakthrough album for Amy was *Age to Age,* which was released in 1982. It dominated the Christian music industry that year and achieved gold status within a year after its release, something no other Christian album had ever done. *(Alleluia, a Praise Gathering for Believers* by the Gaithers and *Music Machine* by Candle both took several years to reach the gold plateau in sales.)

When Amy, her producer Brown Bannister, and management team of Mike Blanton and Dan Harrell began planning the *Age to*

Age album, they decided to attempt a landmark album for the Christian market, akin to the *Tapestry* album by Carole King in the early 1970s. In essence, they wanted to define contemporary Christian music to that audience. Their marketing strategy was to saturate the Christian culture with Amy Grant—something they had been doing in progressive steps with the albums that came before *Age to Age*. They got youth directors and music ministers involved—bringing kids to concerts and hosting "listening" parties. They wanted the whole church world to know about Amy Grant—a monumental task, given the nature of that world—and the success they achieved with *Age to Age* is a direct result of their penetration into the Christian market. (Almost 90 percent of the sales on *Age to Age* came through the Christian bookstores.) Ironically, by creating a landmark album in Christian music, it had an appeal in the pop market from consumers who wanted one contemporary Christian album for their collection or the curious, who wanted to know what all the fuss was about over on the gospel side.

Another irony is that, in the long run, this penetration and saturation of the Christian market helped Sandi Patti more than it did Amy Grant. After the *Age to Age* album, Amy began heading in the direction of pop music and away from the gospel-only customer. Although she still kept her base of support, she also ran into a lot of flack because the gospel audience is very demanding—they want their artists to show a total commitment to gospel music at all times.

Amy Grant created controversy within the Christian culture by taking her Christianity to the secular marketplace. This is anathema to many Christians' view of their faith, which holds that it must separate itself to remain pure. In other words, you don't wear a white dress into a coal mine. But Amy Grant (and her management team) wanted the pop audience to know that Christianity does not have to be stuffy or stale, that it can be fun and relevant to the pop world; they wanted the Christian audience to realize that their music and art could be viable and appealing to the popular culture.

This thrust has seen them achieve great success in the pop market, but it has cost them some of their die-hard Christian supporters.

Sandi Patti does not suffer from this controversy. She is firmly planted in the gospel world—she sees herself as a minister and her career as a ministry—and thus is totally embraced by the gospel world. In a record company advertisement, it says, "Sandi Patti sees her singing as a message God is having her spread around the country, a message of Christian love and hope to people who are hurting emotionally and physically." In a number of interviews, Sandi reiterates, "My audience is the church audience," and she remains committed to "sing for the Lord."

As the gospel community discovered Sandi Patti, there was a position waiting to be filled—that of a singer with a trained voice and a commitment to the Christian community who would sing to the church audience about the Lord. There was no other singer filling that void in 1982, but the marketing of Amy Grant's *Age to Age* album showed the Christian culture how an album and artist could achieve huge sales through exposure and saturation of this marketplace.

23

In the Anderson and Alexandria area, train tracks run all through the towns. Newspaper stories and editorials in the Anderson dailies repeatedly report the accidents—many of them fatal—that have come from trains hitting cars. One such tragedy affected Sandi Patti very deeply because it happened to one of her dearest, closest friends.

Just eight days after Sandi had received her first two Doves in Nashville, twenty-eight-year-old Deborah Cleary was driving west on Taylor Street in Alexandria when she apparently stopped her car on the railroad tracks. The railroad crossing has signs but no flashing lights and when Deborah stopped, the train was only about fifty feet away, moving at twenty-eight miles an hour. According to police, Cleary was aware the train was coming, but had only a few seconds to act—it is not known whether her car stalled or whether she froze in indecision.

The train struck the car broadside and Deborah was thrown about ten feet from the car, suffering a broken neck and internal injuries; she was pronounced dead when she arrived at Community Hospital.

Deborah had sung backup for the Bill Gaither Trio when Sandi was with the group. She also sang backup in the studios, often with Sandi. At the time she died, she was serving as the operations manager for the Barn recording studio. Deborah had lived in Alexandria with her husband Dan, who had worked with the Gaither Trio as a musician.

Sandi said about Debbie: "She was the sort of person you could meet for the first time, and after the first five minutes you felt like you knew her." She continued, "Debbie and I had a lot in common. We sang together; we liked to laugh together; and we went to Weight Watchers together. I would call her and say, 'I've been thinking about this problem and I think the only solution is a banana split.' And Debbie would say, 'Sandi, in our weakness, He is strong.' "

Sandi tells that story on her live album, recorded about ten months after Debbie's death. Sandi had talked to Debbie about doing the live album and wanted Debbie to sing on it with her. There is a deep sadness in Sandi's heart that is heard in her voice when she talks about Debbie Cleary. "God has given us many special friends," she says. "Maybe we need to hug them a little more often and tell them that we love them. Because when the time comes for me, I want my friends and family to know I love them and I want to know I have been loved."

Sandi had a wistful look in her eye when she said about Debbie, "You know, sometimes we don't stop and think about all the really good things going on in our lives until something like this happens. When something tragic happens, it makes you sit back and take stock of the things that are really important, like friendships and other relationships that are special to you. Debbie's friendship was very special to me. I've learned not to take any relationship for granted because you never know if when you say good-bye, hug someone, or say, 'I love you,' it might be the last time. Things can happen beyond our control, so every day has got to be very important . . . Those little things—a phone call, a visit, a lunch date—sometimes seem unimportant, but we shouldn't take them lightly. You never know if you're going to have the opportunity again."

In the gospel music world, 1982 was a year of tragedies. Charlie McPheeters, founder of the Holy Ghost Repair Service in Hollywood, California, and one of the first Jesus rock street evangelists, died on July 31; Ray DeVries, vice president of Lexicon and a key figure in the church music world, died on October 26; and Grady Nutt was killed in a plane crash on November 23 near Vinemont, Alabama. But perhaps the tragedy that struck the contemporary Christian world hardest was the death of Keith Green in an airplane crash near his home at the Last Days Ministries in Lindale, Texas.

Keith Green was a passionate man, considered by many in Christian circles as a prophet, who had a profound impact on contemporary Christian music during his short career. His first album, *For Him Who Has Ears to Hear,* released in 1977, took the gospel world by storm. His second album, *No Compromise,* solidified his position as a Christian musician whose incredible musical gifts only served to give him a platform as a minister who reached deeply into both the Christian and non-Christian cultures.

After Green's first two highly successful albums, he went to his record label and told them he no longer wanted to be on a major label—he wanted to make the albums himself and give them away. This shook the gospel industry down to its sole—most musicians paid for their own records at the beginning of their career because they had to do it in order to get off the ground. And most musicians and singers, despite their pleas to their audience to "give up everything for Jesus," cling tenaciously to their recording contracts, going to great lengths to stay in good graces with their record label. Not so with Keith Green.

More than any other figure, Keith Green established a spiritual integrity with his records, his business ventures, and his life. This integrity would not allow Green to view his Christian music in show-biz terms—he was strictly and unabashedly in gospel music to save other souls and purify his own. Nothing less would do. He was a harsh and difficult critic of the halfhearted and many in Christian music viewed him and his career as what Christian music *should* be.

But most lack Green's courage, commitment, talent, and conviction to take the strong stands he took. Simply put, most people fear for their career—desperately afraid something will destroy it—while Green simply would have no part in a career. By turning his back on all the proper and logical things he should have done, said, or thought, he had a lasting impact on the world he both shunned and embraced when he died at the age of twenty-eight.

The "backmasking" controversy came to the forefront in 1982. Some Christians argued that many rock records had Satanic messages planted in them through a process of "backward masking" or recording messages that could only be decoded by playing the songs backward. A sort of national hysteria developed within the Christian community over this—even though no record player could play a record backward—because it was felt that these subliminal messages took control of young minds everywhere. The obvious fact that nobody had to play any music backward to get messages from all persuasions was not brought up, as witch-hunters such as Paul Crouch, Jr., set up reel-to-reel tape machines to demonstrate their conclusions.

Crouch, who zealously spread this gobbledygook on his parents' Trinity Broadcasting Network, also managed to land on "The Merv Griffin Show," where he exposed these fiendish plots on national television.

Another Crouch—Andrae (no relation to Paul)—raised eyebrows and headlines when he was arrested for cocaine possession in November. Charges were dropped a few days later and Crouch went on to explain that he had lent his car to someone else who apparently left some of the vile stuff in his backseat. Earlier in the year, Crouch had appeared on the CBS-TV show "The Jeffersons" and at the end of the year his name was bandied about to replace Al Green in the Broadway cast of *Your Arms Too Short to Box with God.* Costarring with Green in the two-week run of the play was Patti LaBelle.

The gospel industry, which had proclaimed itself "recession-proof" earlier, found itself in the midst of a major recession—some even called it a depression—in 1982. The surge in 1979, while all about them the secular labels were losing sales, began the splurge of 1980 and 1981 as labels began to get a little fat, leading to the purge of 1982.

The problems began with the fall 1981 Christmas releases. The consumers did not buy as anticipated and the result was a lot of Christmas product still sitting on the shelf after Christmas. January and February are traditionally slow months for record sales and these Christmas albums should have been returned during this time, but two labels threw a curveball at the Christian retailer. Word and Sparrow both announced a retail price increase from $7.98 to $8.98 effective March 1, 1982, with product ordered before that date available at the lower price. Stores wanted to buy before that date and sell later, thereby increasing their mark-up and profits. (Christian bookstores generally do not discount albums the way secular stores do; therefore, albums are sold at "suggested retail price" instead of below it.)

Product began coming back to the labels in record numbers in March because, as bills became due, retailers found the only way they could pay them was by returning product in lieu of cash (the "returned" album was equal in value to the new one). The record industry was stuck with stacks of unsold albums with little if any hope that anyone would ever buy them.

The Benson Company, Sandi's label, was particularly hard hit and they trimmed their staff from 183 to 103 within a few months. According to Wayne Erikson, who was running Benson, they had wanted to be "a Christian communication company" to rival Word and so began to aggressively sign new artists and labels, increase promotion and advertising budgets, and act like a major label.

"We felt that the upsizing of our organization would help us make a greater impact," said Erikson, before admitting that this was a poor management decision. "The answer to the problem is in downsizing and discipline," he concluded. "Not more money [but] doing more with less." At this time, about 40 percent of Benson's product was on back order—the label could not afford to have more pressed to send to the stores—and a number of artists had not been paid royalties.

At the Christian Booksellers' Convention, the mood was glum and reflected cutbacks—Benson spent about a third the amount it usually did and did not sponsor any artist showcases or receptions. The consensus was that Christian labels were going through a shakedown or time of testing and only the fittest would survive. The theme of the CBA that year, "Our Mission: Ministry/Management," seemed especially apropos and label execs began to notice a coming trend—consumers were going for established artists and it was becoming more difficult to break new acts.

Actually, Benson had one of the hottest albums at that time, *Aerobic Celebration,* which began the rush of aerobic albums from Christian labels.

Christian radio was changing and experiencing growing pains along the way. In the summer of 1977, David Benware, a programming consultant for Christian radio, said there could not be an all-contemporary Christian music format because there "wasn't enough product out." That changed dramatically in the next few years and by 1980 there were all-gospel formats on a number of stations. But by 1982, some of these stations had switched formats back to country music, pop, or to the "preaching and teaching" programs they had before.

Prior to this, contemporary Christian music had found its primary outlet through syndicated programs, such as "Joyful Noise" by Paul Baker or shows by Scott Ross and—later—Larry Black. These disc jockeys packaged a show offered to secular stations, which generally played the shows on Sunday mornings. As Christian radio grew, and rock radio was increasingly programmed by consultants who wanted the station to sound the same at 9 A.M. on Sunday as it did at 11:30 P.M. on Friday, these shows departed the airwaves. Too, the FCC no longer required the strict definition of public service it had in the past—a definition that put religious programs in the realm of public service—so stations felt less compelled to put on a gospel show, even if it was gospel rock.

The rise in contemporary Christian radio eased the pain, as more Christian stations programmed more music. The future was beginning to become a little clearer in 1982—program more music on Christian radio, but don't do away with the preaching and teaching programs. And be careful of which preaching and teaching programs you put on the air. This assured stations they would attract a larger audience. It also helped that by 1982 there was much more contemporary Christian product available and that producers and artists were attuned to quality in recording, so the music would sound as good on the air as a secular station's records.

The record industry in general has been characterized by its adherence to "gut reaction" in making marketing decisions, but as market research began to dominate American business and number crunchers emerged as powerful leaders, the record industry began to look at ways to measure itself. The results dispelled a number of old myths (such as kids buy all the music) and created a new awareness of the market. The Christian record industry, while lagging behind the secular industry (which did its first market research in 1976) began to look at itself in terms of numbers in 1982 and uncovered some interesting facts.

Mediamark Research, Inc., (MRI) conducted a survey for Bread 'n Honey Records and sampled twenty thousand homes. Its conclusion: "Christian buying habits and daily activities are, for the most part, not that different from anyone else's. The big difference comes in how a Christian perceives the world around him."

This survey found that 44 percent of those who listen to religious radio are between the ages of eighteen and thirty-four, with the prime range between twenty-five and thirty-four, while those over forty-five years old accounted for 40 percent of the market. (The previous myth had been that the only people who listened to religious radio were blue-haired old ladies.) They discovered two and a half million people who listen to religious radio (although a number within the gospel industry said that figure was low) and that 65 percent were married, 20 percent were single, 39 percent were parents, and 15 percent were either widowed or divorced.

Of those in the survey who said they listened to religious radio on a regular basis, 30 percent purchased beer within the last year, 88 percent frequented fast-food restaurants, and 67 percent did not drink coffee. Their favorite television shows were "The Jeffersons," "Three's Company," "60 Minutes," "CHIPs," "Dallas," "The Love Boat," "Happy Days," "M*A*S*H," and "Alice." Two thirds owned a domestic car (and tended to buy American products) and shopped at discount department stores. Forty-one percent said they did not contribute to their church during the past year, but 38 percent said they did contribute to a political candidate. Finally—the most alarming statistic—74 percent who said they listened to religious radio did not buy any albums during the previous year.

It wasn't all bad news in 1982—there was plenty to crow about, too. Amy Grant and Gary Chapman got married on June 19; in California, at the Crystal Cathedral, John Cruse of the Cruse Family married Jancie Archer of the Archers. And over in Singapore, the first Christian Artists Seminar was held, joining the ones in Estes Park, Colorado, and De Bron, Holland, in uniting Christian musicians in various parts of the world.

The Christian rock band Petra, Wes Yoder's Dharma Agency, the National Gospel Radio Seminar, Maranatha! Music, and several other ministries reached the ten-year milestone and celebrated a decade in the Christian culture carved from the Jesus Revolution in the early 1970s.

24

There are five attributes of a great musical artist: (1) they have talent; (2) they have charisma; (3) they are competitive; (4) they have a burning desire to perform live; and (5) they have a certain uniqueness.

Most performers do not possess all of these attributes; those that possess all five are in a special category. But even having all this is not enough—management must play a key role. It is no surprise that the two major stars in gospel music—Sandi Patti and Amy Grant—both have excellent management teams. Nothing just "happens" and, for a performer and artist, it is the manager who is the instigator, the catalyst, and the visionary who makes the career move forward.

The key element between an artist and a manager is trust. The artist must trust the manager totally with career decisions. Most people are not "manageable" in this sense—they will not trust someone else to make major decisions for them about their life and career. Since Sandi's manager is her husband, a major barrier for trust is removed. Still, it takes a very special kind of trust, enabling the artist to sing and perform while letting the manager do what he does, that often separates the few top acts from a host of those who never make it to the top.

It is especially difficult to find someone "manageable" in gospel music. After all, the Christian premise is that each person must communicate with God directly, must follow their own individual calling. Therefore, a spiritual bond must exist between gospel artists and their managers as well as a contract. The artist must believe God is working through the manager and by following his decisions, they are also following God's will. Most artists rebel at this concept.

Sandi Patti and Amy Grant have another important attribute in common: They were both given an early platform to exhibit their talents. For Amy, this came from her family, who was wealthy enough to hire an independent record promoter for her first album and to subsidize her first tours when she took out a full band. This allowed her the privilege of breaking new ground—giving audiences a top-notch Christian show—without the necessity of making money being an influence on major career decisions. For Sandi, it was being placed by Bill Gaither in a prominent spot on his shows in front of large receptive audiences. This allowed her to go first-class from the beginning, to have her talent exposed in major venues, and to not be restricted by lack of money or opportunity. Still, it must be emphasized that you cannot buy success in gospel music or any other field of entertainment. Yes, these two women had finances and opportunities, but they had the talent to deliver the goods.

Managers take care of the myriad of details in an artist's life, allowing the artist freedom. The most frustrating thing for an artist is having to make daily business decisions, arrange press interviews, answer correspondence, maintain record company relations, stay in contact with concert promoters, and other things that are necessary to maintain a successful career. For Sandi Patti, she simply depends upon John to take care of all these matters—and it is done.

Another vital function of the manager is to "shield" an artist. When a manager makes a decision, everyone cannot be happy. Those who are not happy can always blame the manager—he can be the bad guy—while the artist can remain above the fray. It is convenient for the artist, in awkward situations, to say the manager must make the decision, even when their own input is vital and perhaps decisive. John Helvering plays the role of scapegoat for Sandi, so she can be at home relaxing with Anna or studying the Bible and meditating while John is on the front line. She is not worn down from the day-to-day decisions and thus is able to be more effective onstage because she comes there fresh. It gives her a freedom because she is comfortable knowing that she will not be in sticky situations, that all the details have been taken care of, that someone is watching out for her best interests.

It seems John and Sandi had been working toward a manager-artist relationship as well as a husband-wife relationship since their marriage in 1978. At first, John organized the concerts, made sure the sound was right, and tied up all the loose ends, so Sandi only had to worry about singing. But he was also making business contacts, setting up the books, and securing a recording contract for her. By mid-1981, Sandi had several albums out and was performing with the Bill Gaither Trio as well as the Imperials and John had plans to have a full-time operating agency by summer 1982. However, when Sandi was awarded her first Dove awards, the phone immediately went crazy, ringing for five hundred requests for bookings in the following six months. John scrambled to find a full-time secretary and did what he could to make ends meet. Sandi's role as an opening act came to an end while she increased her solo performances from about one hundred a year to around two hundred.

In June 1982 John's brother Bob, who had been teaching high school in Indianapolis, joined the firm to handle all the bookings. Bob screens all the calls, then discusses them with John before deciding which ones to take. Their decisions are generally based on which appearances are most beneficial careerwise, are financially sound, and are routed so that Sandi makes best use of geography in her appearances, never covering too many miles between shows. Also added to the staff in the summer of 1982 were Linda Mason as director of publicity and promotion and Amy Yahnig as executive assistant to John. True to form, all of the employees were Anderson College graduates.

Later others were added, including Don Boyer, who solicits press coverage for Sandi and makes sure that an attractive press kit, with up-to-date photos, a biography, and press clippings, is maintained and made available to key media representatives. The growth of the company came relatively quickly—by the end of 1986, there were seventeen on the office staff.

Sandi has been honest about some of the problems facing an artist when her manager is also her husband. "I wouldn't be honest if I said every day is rosy," she said, "because it's not. But every day as husband and wife isn't rosy, especially when you compound the personal relationship with a professional one on top of it. Another artist may have a disagreement with her manager and she can grumble about it to her husband and say that she never wants to see the manager again. But me? I've got to go home and cook dinner for mine! So there are definitely some tough times that we wade through, but we keep communicating, and sometimes that communication comes from listening. Again, I think the good far outweighs the bad."

Sandi has never been disturbed about the "business" aspects of her message and career. "I feel so very confident about what I would like to say that selling has never been a question for me," Sandi said. "I look for songs that communicate—that's my criterion. A song might mean something for me, but is it going to mean something to the person listening in his car? Is it going to communicate there? I continually ask, in whatever it is, 'Lord, is there eternity in this? If there is, I want with all my heart to be a part of it. If there isn't, please, please guide me.' I continue to ask that, whether it be the Johnny Carson show, choosing songs for an album, or going on vacation with my family. 'Is there eternal value in this?' I may not always voice it that way, but inside, that's the question I ask.

"The more people you have to communicate with, the more the logistics of communicating your message becomes a problem. That's when the business aspect begins to play a big part. We all have to be good stewards of the gifts God has given us, not only as musicians, but also in management and in the production of records. That's all part of communicating the message.

"Yes, it can get out of balance if the music becomes only a way to make money. I continue to ask the Lord, 'Help me not to be sidetracked. Help me to keep my focus.' Each individual artist has to work through that himself."

And that is an interesting and admirable quality about Sandi Patti—even though she has grown rich by recording and performing Christian music, money has never been the factor motivating her career decisions. Indeed, it seems almost like a by-product of her efforts rather than a motivation.

25

Sandi Patti signed another contract with the Benson Company in late 1982. This new contract gave her more control of her recordings and career and a higher royalty rate. Sandi had put together a good artist development team and Benson, despite their problems, was a strong part of it.

Sandi recorded a live album January 16 in Lakeland, Florida. This concert, which became the *Live . . . More Than Wonderful* album, showed an artist who was emerging as a powerful solo performer. This album captures Sandi in a setting that showcases her appeal. It allowed her to do her big hits (a live album is often a greatest hits package in a different format) and to tie in her live show with her recorded work. It also became a milestone in contemporary Christian music because, with this album, the inspirational or church audience market was "discovered" and began to dominate gospel music.

The album begins with Sandi singing a line a cappella, then the announcer's voice, followed by a big overture for an up-tempo song whose message is essentially that the believer is "in Christ" and Christians are His voice or spokesmen.

Sandi's renditions of "Jesus Loves Me" are cute and enlightening because she uses this song to show her influences—Karen Carpenter, Barbra Streisand, formal voice training, and finally as a member of the church. It is light and humorous and probably the highlight of the album, capturing on tape the feeling and mood she captured in concert.

Side One finishes with "Upon This Rock," another song that affirms that Christians are set apart from the rest of the world. The believer sees with "spirit eyes," while others miss or deny the "priceless truth" that only the Christian can "know and recognize." For this, the Christian is given eternal life and the church on earth is founded on him—a tall order and big responsibility, but one that the Christian gladly accepts.

On Side Two, Larnelle Harris is introduced and sings a duet with Sandi. "More Than Wonderful" says that what the singers feel about Jesus cannot be described because He is more than wonderful to them. It is a statement of love—the love of man for God—and presents one of the roles the Christian sees for himself here on earth: to be a lover of Jesus.

The album closes with "We Shall Behold Him." No live performance of Sandi's would be complete without this song, so it is especially appropriate on her live album. But the inclusion of this song also allows Sandi to put the *Love Overflowing* album behind her—an album that was not up to par with her more recent albums—and give fans "We Shall Behold Him" on an album where the material is more in line with the message in that song. Hearing it sung live, one is again captured by the power, beauty, and majesty of the song and Sandi's voice—it will always be a song that "defines" her.

In a review, *CCM*'s Paul Baker wrote that the album "doesn't necessarily qualify as a classic . . . but preserved between some lighter moments of fellowship lie some distinctly beautiful and worshipful renditions of several magnificent songs." Baker concluded, "God has given Sandi Patti an immense store of talent, but with albums such as this one, everyone becomes the beneficiary."

Baker was only wrong on one count: The album soon proved to be a classic and—with it—Sandi exploded as a major force in Christian music. The key word here is "force," because this album moved her up from being a "star" and winner of some gospel awards to a major influence in the field.

When the 1983 Doves rolled around, Sandi was scheduled to perform. She was also up again for Female Vocalist, against Amy Grant, Tanya Goodman, Barbara Mandrell, and Kelly Nelon Thompson and for Artist of the Year, along with the Cathedrals, Amy Grant, Deanna McClary, and the Rex Nelon Singers. "We Shall Behold Him" was again up for Song of the Year honors, as was "How Majestic Is Your Name," while Sandi's *Lift Up the Lord* album was also contending.

Sandi won two Doves—for Female Vocalist and Inspirational Album, but it was clearly Amy Grant's year. The success of the *Age to Age* album led Amy to capture the Artist of the Year honor, as well as generating three other Dove winners (including Song of the Year for "El Shaddai").

The show, hosted by Pat Boone, was a special evening for Bill Gaither, who was inducted into the Gospel Music Hall of Fame. Sandi and Amy shared the duty of performing the songs nominated for Song of the Year. During a press gathering after the show where she posed for photographers, Sandi lifted her two Doves and said, "These are very heavy. I'm always surprised to win."

The Grammy Awards netted Sandi her first nomination—along with Andrae Crouch, the Imperials, Reba Rambo, and Amy Grant in the Best Gospel Performance, Contemporary, category. But she walked home empty-handed from that ceremony—Amy won for her *Age to Age* album.

The 1983 Grammys were a disappointment for many contemporary Christian fans, who were getting accustomed to a healthy dose of their favorite music and artists on the network show. Gospel Grammy winners Al Green, Barbara Mandrell, and the Blackwood Brothers were given their awards during the pretelecast ceremonies. Except for Ricky Skaggs and the Masters V singing "I'll Fly Away" and Little Richard rocking out with "Joy Joy Joy," there were not any performances from contemporary Christian artists.

At the beginning of the year, "How Majestic Is Your Name"

was on airplay charts; in May "More Than Wonderful" made its entry; and in July "Upon This Rock" debuted. At the end of the year, "O Magnify the Lord" (from her Christmas album) entered. This shows that Sandi was now being heard regularly on Christian radio.

In the middle of the year, *CCM* created *MusicLine,* a trade magazine with detailed charts for the gospel industry, while *CCM* remained a consumer publication and the album charts listed only the top fifty sellers, with no breakdowns for categories. There were also no more airplay charts in *CCM*.

At the end of the year, Sandi had four albums—*More Than Wonderful* at number two, *Lift Up the Lord* at thirteen, *Love Overflowing* at twenty-seven, and *The Gift Goes On* at forty-four; on the sales chart, Amy Grant had three albums (including *Age to Age,* which was still number one, eighteen months after its release), the Imperials had three, Petra had two, Keith Green had three, and B. J. Thomas had two albums. Michael W. Smith—writer of "How Majestic Is Your Name"—had his debut album at number seven, while Russ Taff's debut solo album was at number five, and it was becoming apparent that the Christian music industry was being dominated by a relative handful of artists. And Sandi Patti, with a 20 percent share of the charts, was beginning to lead the pack.

At the end of 1983, Sandi Patti and Amy Grant continued to dominate the gospel industry—but there was beginning to be a noticeable difference that reflected the two directions contemporary Christian music was heading. Amy had just received a gold album for her *Age to Age* album and was beginning to reach toward the pop world, whose media was already beginning to cover her. Sandi was dominating the gospel world—as indicated by her having more songs on the charts at the end of 1983 than any other gospel act—but her sales were not yet in the same league as Amy's. However, Sandi was intent upon staying with the church audience. Ironically, both of these two decisions would pay off handsomely for each.

The first cover story on Sandi in *CCM* came out in January but, because of an error, said "1982" on the masthead instead of "1983." Written by Jim Hall and titled "Sandi's Down-to-Earth, But Her Music Is Heavenly," the article noted, "By Sandi's own admission, she is not one who is particularly attracted to 'glamour,' though this usually warm, glowing, and animated lady does cut a striking figure onstage wearing a flowing Qiana dress."

In the article, Sandi talked about her music, her ministry, and her awards, saying, "I do have a tremendous responsibility now. When I received the Dove Awards, it was like my peers were saying to me, 'We feel like what you're doing is worthwhile. We're behind you and we're counting on you to do your part to share about the Lord.' I have an opportunity to share some life-changing concepts with people. That's scary, but it's also exciting to know that for some reason the Lord has given me this responsibility. I'm sure not taking it lightly."

Sandi was also candid in this article about some fears and drawbacks to a successful career in Christian music. "Sometimes I can get so busy actually doing the things for the Lord that I can get bogged down by it all," she said. "It's kind of like driving a gorgeous Cadillac; if you don't have gas in it, it doesn't do you much good. I can run and run and run, but if I don't get refueled and get that renewed commitment daily, then the other things I'm doing are not going to have a lasting value."

Talking about her performances, Sandi told Charles Phillips, who did a feature on her for the *Saturday Evening Post,* "I feel that you have to get the people's attention before you can say anything of value. That's where the entertainment part comes in. But I don't want it only to be entertainment. I want people to leave with something that they'll think about for several days. Audiences vary; in some situations I have to go out and convince them that I'm O.K., legitimate, and not trying to take their money and run. I have to kind of win them over."

She found that fame sometimes brings other problems as well, such as young girls idolizing her. "Too many people think that they want to be like this person or that person. I have a lot of young girls come up to me and say, 'My goal is to be just like you.' I tell them, 'But I want you to be what the Lord wants you to be. Strive for something better than to be just like me; strive for what the Lord wants you to be.' "

Discussing her future, Sandi told *CCM* that she "honestly" didn't know, but hoped to "be involved with music for many years to come, because I think it's a really neat way to communicate the Gospel. But if, say, ten years or so down the road I'm involved with teaching or in some kind of behind-the-scenes aspect of the industry, I'll enjoy that, too."

Sandi also reiterated her desire at this time to do some teaching, saying, "At some point in my life, I'd like to work with special education students, maybe in music therapy, perhaps with deaf or autistic children . . . I feel that music can sometimes break down walls when maybe just words can't. I'm just really excited about the Lord's using music to heal people's lives and it would be wonderful to be used by Him in that way all the time."

26

Sandi Patti's career has always been given an added boost because of her willingness and desire to tie in with other organizations and artists. She does this by performing duets, by appearing in advertisements for others, through endorsements, and by singing on albums that are not her own.

On the *Love Overflowing* album there are two duets—one with Russ Taff on "Home of the Lord" and the other with Phil Johnson on "When the Time Comes." On the *Live . . . More Than Wonderful* album, her duet with Larnelle Harris achieved major success. The duets with Taff and Harris would appear on compilation albums released by Benson during 1983; the "Home of the Lord" would be a track on an album of contemporary duets, while "More Than Wonderful" would be a cut on an album of inspirational duets.

At the beginning of 1983, Benson released *We Shall Behold Him: The Musical,* which consists of a number of Dottie Rambo songs. On this album, Sandi's version of "We Shall Behold Him" was the major track.

With her live performances, she kept her association with the Bill Gaither Trio, performing with them during their spring tour, which covered twenty-four cities. In the fall of the year, she was the opening act for the Imperials on their tour, which included a jaunt to Australia and New Zealand.

Already, Sandi was receiving international exposure. In 1982 she had attended the Christian Artists Seminar in Asia and performed with Dino in Djakarta, Indonesia; Hong Kong; Taipei, Taiwan; Seoul, Korea; and Osaka, Japan. In 1983 Sandi would appear in Amsterdam at the World Evangelism Conference sponsored by Billy Graham and do a short tour of Canada.

She again performed at the Christian Artists Seminar in the Rockies in Estes Park, Colorado, at the Gaithers' Praise Gathering in Indianapolis, at the National Religious Broadcasters' Convention in Washington, and at three Jesus Festivals during the summer.

The first big Christian festival was Explo '72 at the Cotton Bowl in Dallas, which was attended by an estimated 180,000 people. Performances by Johnny Cash, Kris Kristofferson, Larry Norman, Connie Smith, Mike Warnke, Reba Rambo, Andrae Crouch and the Disciples, Barry McGuire, and others highlighted a week filled with seminars and other festivities. But the real roots for Christian festivals lay in pop festivals, such as the Newport Jazz Festival in the 1960s, the Monterey Pop Festival in 1967, and, of course, the granddaddy of them all, Woodstock in 1969.

In 1973 the first festival with a major emphasis on contemporary Christian music was organized by Harold Zimmerman and held in a Pennsylvania potato field. Called Jesus '73, the event continued annually. Jesus '77 came from a group of Christian businessmen who formed a nonprofit organization called Jesus Ministries in 1976. It was held on Agape Camp Farm, a 280-acre year-round retreat center with a fifteen-room motel, a bookstore, and grocery. It also has a pond, where a number of baptisms have occurred since the inception of these festivals.

Praise '74, Salt '75, Fishnet '75, Sonshine, Lodestone, Road Home Celebration, and a number of others have all followed this trend. Even amusement parks have come on this bandwagon with Knott's Berry Farm in Buena Park, California, providing the most successful example, beginning with their Maranatha! Night celebrations in 1974. Sandi has always been aware of the appeal of festivals and wanted to sing for these audiences.

Satellite Concerts, sponsored by Youth with a Vision, a ministry of Word of Faith Outreach Center in Dallas, began a concert series in their local church that was transmitted live via satellite to over 650 churches, where audiences could gather and watch. Sandi appeared on this network with Larnelle Harris and on "Serve the Lord," a program hosted by Terry and Cheryl Blackwood on the Trinity Broadcasting Network.

In another attempt to capture the television market, Sandi had her spring concert at Anderson College taped by the broadcasting department. The result was fifty-eight minutes and thirty seconds of videotape that those involved thought fit for national distribution. Taped at Byrum Hall on the campus, the show was recorded by students and faculty, headed by Don Boggs, a broadcasting instructor, and featured eleven songs by Sandi, including one with a children's choir, as well as duets with Steve Green and her brother Craig.

In June and July, Sandi was in Great Circle Sound Studio, the Benson Company's recording facility, to record her Christmas album. There was a Christmas tree put up in the studio, a gift exchange, and the air-conditioning was cranked up to help those involved get in the Christmas spirit. The result was *The Gift Goes On,* released that fall.

There are several medleys of Christmas classics, as well as new songs, such as "Worship the King" and "O Magnify the Lord," on the album. "The Gift Goes On," with a chorus reminiscent of José Feliciano's "Feliz Navidad," introduces the concept that Jesus is the "gift" God has given to man.

"Christmas Was Meant for Children," an old song from Fred Waring's publishing catalogue, creates a mood reminiscent of "Chestnuts Roasting on an Open Fire."

The album closes with a song that Sandi must have sung along with a Karen Carpenter record back in school—"Have Yourself a Merry Little Christmas"—and Sandi sounds as if she has every one of Karen's inflections down perfectly. It is a nice ending for this album, and is a gift from Sandi to her fans and listeners—a wish that everyone's Christmas will be as bright and warm as the Helverings'.

In the December issue of *CCM,* Amy's and Sandi's Christmas albums were reviewed on the same page. The review on Sandi is positive: "From the lyrics, to the orchestration, on down to the letter from Sandi's parents inside the album jacket, *The Gift Goes On* indeed draws the listener to the true spirit of Christmas." *MusicLine* said, "Retailers had just better hope they have the supply to meet the demand" and other periodicals also lauded the album.

But record reviews were not the most important things on Sandi's mind during the Christmas season in 1983. This Christmas there was a wonderful present growing inside her: She and John were expecting their first child in the spring. The feeling gave Sandi a cozy warmth and she must have smiled as she tried to imagine Christmas with a child in their family. And she must also have felt a joy carrying the unborn child much greater than even the joy that Christmas always brings. Yes, this would be a *very* special Christmas!

27

The Recording Industry Association of America, an organization that certifies gold and platinum albums, reported in 1983 that gospel sales accounted for 6 percent of recorded product in the United States, up from 4 percent retail and 5 percent direct-marketing share reported in 1981.

Gospel industry spokespersons had indicated that gospel outsold jazz and classical. However, the RIAA disagreed, saying classical outsold gospel in direct marketing (sales by mail) and its share of the industry sales is larger. An inherent problem here in measuring gospel sales against a category such as jazz or classical is that the latter forms reach basically one audience with one kind of music (although there is, obviously, much variety within these musics), but gospel reaches different audiences with an extremely wide range of music—from Southern quartets to black gospel choirs to heavy metal gospel and everything in between.

Word Records commissioned a survey of Christian radio that showed that contemporary Christian radio, a relatively young industry (about eight years old then), was struggling for a tiny share of the radio audience.

Generally, Christian radio stations have smaller antennas and power assignments, making it more difficult to sound good and reach a wide geographical area. Using Arbitron survey results (Arbitron is a company that measures rating and shares of radio stations in various markets), this survey discovered that only five of the top fifteen markets in the United States have a Christian station with enough of an audience to show up in Arbitron's published results.

Of the contemporary Christian stations that did show up, most had shares in the 1.1 to 1.5 range. (Ratings are based on the percentage of those listening to a particular station measured against the total population of an area; share indicates the number listening to a particular station measured against the population listening to radio at that time.)

This survey also showed that 83 percent of Christian stations take requests, which means that since a very narrow segment of the audience ever calls in to request a song, the station is often at the requester's mercy. But overall, most stations were programmed according to the personal tastes of the music or programming director, who believed either that the Lord told him to play a particular song at a particular time or that "the audience wants to hear what I want to hear." About 43 percent of those surveyed had no set rotation of songs.

A major problem at Christian radio stations was music—or, rather, the lack of it. The survey reported that the average day at a Christian radio station was 18.2 hours, with music played an average of 8.2 hours and the bulk of the remaining 10 hours a day made up of taped preaching and teaching programs.

Another problem at radio stations, from the record company's point of view, was the issue of singles. The secular marketplace had realized that by having several hit singles from an album, the life of an album could be a year or more in the marketplace. But the Christian programmer was used to receiving albums, which he aired heavily, so the several most popular cuts would become overplayed after three months, causing demand for another album. In the past, gospel artists had been used to releasing two, three, or four albums a year, while secular artists were used to releasing two a year. (The Beatles used to release an album every six months.) Obviously, this was not good for saturating a market and maximizing profits, so record companies were looking for ways to prolong the life of an album through singles strategically spaced throughout the year. Christian radio was reluctant to change, but was beginning to realize that if they were going to get better shares and ratings in their market and attract advertising (local, regional, and national), then they would need to play the hottest songs more often.

The Word report concluded that Christian radio was doing poorly, with about 1.6 percent of the national marketplace, ahead of only "Spanish-language programming, solid-gold formats, classical and jazz stations."

Contemporary Christian Music did a survey that profiled their readers and discovered a music-loving group. Almost 60 percent of the respondents said they bought ten or more albums each year and 31.2 percent said they purchased more than sixteen albums a year; 75.8 percent said they listen to music more than ten hours a week and most said that what the artist was saying was more important than the quality of the recording.

The *CCM* survey also showed that 94.7 percent of respondents said they attended a concert in the past year, 47.6 percent said they attended more than four, and 7 percent attended more than eleven. Most (72.8 percent) listened to secular music and attended concerts by secular artists, but there was a hard-core group of Christian consumers (27.2 percent) who stated they *only* listen to Christian music.

This survey also showed that 94.9 percent of those responding were under thirty-four, with 57.6 percent under twenty-five; 69.9 percent were male and most (61.6 percent) were single.

All of these facts and figures helped clarify the Christian consumer in the marketplace and pointed out some interesting trends that the Christian music industry would capitalize on in the future. There was a sizable core of young Christians who liked contemporary Christian music and who were active buyers, providing a potential for Christian record companies to achieve big sales figures on albums, if only they could convince radio to program singles in high rotation. Both of these trends would help play a major role in the success of Sandi Patti, whose audience consisted of a large number of young people and college students and whose album sales benefited directly from the promotion of singles, beginning with "We Shall Behold Him."

In news from the music world, 1983 is remembered as the year when one of Sandi Patti's major musical influences, Karen Carpenter, died on February 4. It was also the year Michael Jackson sold twenty million copies of *Thriller,* the hot movie was *Flashdance,* and noted Christian speaker Corrie ten Boom, author of *The Hiding Place,* died.

28

Winning the Dove for Female Vocalist of the Year was getting to be an annual event for Sandi Patti; she won it for the third consecutive time at the fifteenth annual Dove Awards in 1984.

These Doves were televised for the first time and aired on cable, over the Christian Broadcasting Network, after a number of years of concentrated effort by members of the GMA to get the show on television.

Sandi was nominated with Cynthia Clawson, Tanya Goodman, Amy Grant, Michelle Pillar, and Kelly Nelon Thompson in the Female Vocalist category. In the Inspirational Album category, two of her albums—*Live . . . More Than Wonderful* and *The Gift Goes On*—competed against each other and against albums by the New Gaither Vocal Band, Kelly Nelon Thompson, and Phil Driscoll. In the Design category, her album *Live . . . More Than Wonderful* was nominated and in the Song of the Year category, two songs she popularized, "More Than Wonderful" and "Upon This Rock," were both nominated. And, in the all-important Artist of the Year category, Sandi was nominated, along with Amy Grant, Dino Kartsonakis, Petra, and John Michael Talbot.

At the end of the evening, Sandi carried home three Doves. In addition to Female Vocalist, her album *Live . . . More Than Wonderful* won in its category, "More Than Wonderful" won Song of the Year honors, and the writer of "More Than Wonderful," Lanny

Wolfe, took home the Dove for Songwriter of the Year. Sandi and Larnelle Harris received a standing ovation when they performed "More Than Wonderful."

The very pregnant Sandi sobbed when she received the Artist of the Year award, saying, "I'm in shock. I can't believe I won the entertainer of the year." Later, backstage, she told reporters and photographers, "My next big award is due in two months. The month of May may be more exciting for me than what happened tonight."

Amy Grant, who many had predicted to be the big winner after her year-long success with the gold album *Age to Age,* received only one Dove—for Design of her Christmas album. The message sent was clear: The Doves are the domain of the gospel world, which is dominated by the church audience. Lanny Wolfe reflected on this after his Doves, saying, "I think there's more of an awareness of what's happening in the body of Christ. Sometimes we get caught up in the charts and radio airplay and all those things are perhaps necessary and important, but when I write a song I'm not thinking about radio airplay because I know there's an awful lot of people who meet on Sunday morning and there's an awful lot of churches who need a vehicle to worship God, so I think God has given me a special ministry for the body of Christ."

Sandi expressed a similar sentiment, "I think church people are becoming more aware of what's going on. That's where I feel my ministry is directed right now—to the church body."

At the Grammys, Sandi received two nominations. *The Gift Goes On* was nominated in the Female Gospel Vocal category and "More Than Wonderful" was nominated in the Group Gospel Vocal category. By the end of the evening, Sandi had won her first Grammy, with Larnell Harris, for their duet "More Than Wonderful."

At the beginning of the year, Sandi had four albums on the *CCM* top fifty sales chart: *More Than Wonderful, The Gift Goes On, Lift Up the Lord,* and *Love Overflowing.* The top position on this chart had been held by Amy Grant's *Age to Age* until May, when her *Straight Ahead* album debuted at number one and replaced it. But in December, Amy lost her grip on the number one position. That's when *Songs from the Heart,* which entered in November, moved into the number one slot. This was followed by Amy's two albums—*Straight Ahead* and *Age to Age*—while *Live . . . More Than Wonderful* was at number four.

During this year, Evie released a collection of standards titled *Hymns* and the Imperials released *The Imperials Sing the Classics,* another collection of hymns. It was becoming apparent that the record buyers were ready for the ageless, timeless hymns. (In pop music, Linda Ronstadt and Willie Nelson had shown the appeal of old pop standards with their *Lush Life* and *Stardust* albums.)

There were already enough advance orders placed at the Christian Booksellers' Association convention to assure the success of *Songs from the Heart.* When it was released, Benson sent out a lot of merchandising material, such as posters, mobiles, and stickers, to display in Christian bookstores. The company also placed four-color ads that fall in *CCM, MusicLine, Charisma,* and *Christian Life* magazines and made money available for radio advertising.

The cover of the album is tinted pink and features a close-up of Sandi, turned and looking straight at the camera with a slight smile. It is attractive, soft, warm, and very feminine. Inside is perhaps Sandi's most personal and revealing album.

The first single is "Sing to the Lord," which is reminiscent of Amy Grant's "Sing Your Praise to the Lord" intro from her *Age to Age* album. "Cradle Song" is a ballad about the joys of having a child. Since this was the year of motherhood for Sandi, the appeal of a song like this is obvious.

"Wonderful Lord" is a light, breezy number that presents the theology that we should love God (and be Christians) because of what God can do for us, a recurring theme in the Christian culture.

Side One closes with "Via Dolorosa," the song of the Crucifixion in which Sandi's role is that of the narrator, telling this picturesque story in a way that visualizes the scene. The big show opening again accents the drama as the monologue unfolds.

"Pour on the Power" on Side Two is a snappy, almost "novelty," tune that features some excellent and catchy background vocal work. "Glorious Morning" is another Resurrection song and it is becoming obvious at this point in Sandi's career that she has several favorite themes. She likes the Resurrection story songs and does them with lots of dramatic urgency and intensity; she likes the "getting to Heaven and seeing how marvelous it is" songs; and she likes the straightforward "praise" songs that, lyrically, simply state Christianity in its traditional—though most flattering—terms.

"The Stage Is Bare" closes the album and is an interesting song because it revealingly presents the dilemma of being a Christian artist and celebrity. Sandi uses her Streisand voice and the scene is similar to one from *A Star Is Born* when the singer confronts an empty stage. It is a piano ballad and Sandi finds herself alone with God, a frightening as well as comforting position for her to be in. She admits that it is easy to be a Christian with so many other Christians around, but it is much more difficult when no one else is watching. It is this dilemma that causes so many Christians to be hypocrites—presenting one face to the congregation but wearing a totally different one away from the crowd of saints. In this song, Sandi recognizes the dilemma and fights against it—she earnestly desires to be a Christian no matter who is watching, and ends the song with an old hymn, "I Need Thee Every Hour."

The back cover of *Songs from the Heart* reveals several interesting things. First, there is a picture of the new family and Sandi's dedication of the album to her new daughter. In the credits, Sandi is listed as coproducer, which shows her emerging role in the studio. Finally John Helvering is listed as executive producer, a credit that also began after their new contract with Benson and first appeared on the *Live . . . More Than Wonderful* album. This shows an increasing amount of power from the Helverings concerning their recorded product—now they have more control about what goes on an album, how it is packaged, how it is produced and arranged, and how it will be promoted. It is another step toward the Helverings having complete control over Sandi's career and indicates they —not the record company—are now calling the shots.

29

It was a cool and overcast day in Anderson, Indiana, and it rained a little. The newspaper headlines told of the Persian Gulf conflict between Iran and Iraq, but the biggest news on May 22, 1984, for Sandi Patti was that she was finally a *mother.* Anna Elizabeth Helvering was born in St. John's Hospital in Anderson.

"As long as I can remember, I have always wanted to be a mother." This sentiment probably sums up Sandi better than anything else she—or anyone else—has ever said about her. To be a mother. To love a child, to have a family of her own, to be loved and needed by a new life. This is the dream of Sandi Patti that came true that spring day in Indiana when there was a touch of chill in the air and a bit of rain in the sky. It is a day Sandi will never forget, will always cherish because, more than all the awards and honors and filled auditoriums of admiring throngs, a mother is what Sandi Patti really wants to be.

Anna changed Sandi's life personally and professionally. Sandi said, after the birth of her daughter, "One of the main things Anna has made me realize is the seriousness of life. Although I've always taken my relationship with the Lord seriously, it has taken on new importance because I realize it is now my responsibility to pass on my faith to a new little person."

Sandi had also always taken her marriage seriously, "but I understand now that there is a little girl who is counting on her mother and father to stay together and give her the kind of love and upbringing that she needs."

Sandi took her new role to heart and set about being the best mother she could be. She thought about her role as a career woman and mother to Anna. "I can't just blow into her life one day and out the next," she said. "I need to get involved now in the things that will affect my daughter's life twenty years from now. This is the time, when she's too young to go to school, that we will do the most traveling. Afterward, it'll be summers and weekends. It's not fair for her to grow up in an unrealistic environment with no one she can really relate to. When she's in college, I don't want her to say she never went to elementary school because she was studying on the road. I don't want her—or any of the kids we want to have in the future—to miss out on those beautiful experiences."

Sandi has always respected her own mother, admiring the way she treats her father, always knowing what he wants, anticipating his needs. Sandi longs to be the same kind of wife for John. She admits that her mother inspires her. "I've never stopped wanting to be like her," she said.

Professionally, Anna had a great impact on Sandi the singer. The new mom admitted, "I'm also thinking even more seriously about what I say in my concerts. I can't just *say* how I feel about the Lord; He's got to be so much a part of my life that I can live out my commitment to Him even when I'm changing diapers or getting up in the middle of the night with Anna when she won't stop crying." She added, "[Anna's birth] made me realize what a tremendous responsibility has been placed in the hands of John and me, a responsibility not just to sing the words that are in my songs, but to live them out."

Sandi told *CCM*'s Davin Seay, "I'm a real homebody. There was a time when I wondered if I wasn't going to get a station wagon, or a chance to go to the post office, or to drop the kids off at school, or do any of those suburban things I've always wanted . . . Sometimes I do feel torn, I'm so happy we can take her with us now. She rolled over for the first time in Spokane, and I cried, thinking how happy I was that I was there to see it and didn't have to hear about it from a baby-sitter over the phone . . . because that's the last 'first time' forever."

Already, Sandi was gearing her future plans around Anna. Looking ahead, she said, "My husband and I will face tremendous challenges in planning our schedules so that we have good quality time both at home and on the road, but we feel that with enough advance preparation we can do it. When Anna reaches kindergarten age, we will stay home more because it will be important for her to get a normal school education. During those years, we'll limit our travel to summertime. We don't plan, unless the Lord directs us otherwise, to ever stop traveling completely."

Sandi has learned a lot about mixing motherhood with her career as a Christian singer from Gloria Gaither. "No one loves family like Gloria does," said Sandi. "This became especially meaningful to me when I knew I was going to have a child of my own. I'd ask her, 'How do you do this? How do you do that?' She told me over and over that family is more important than career, but there's a way to do both. She suggested that when John and I travel we take the baby with us for the first four or five years.

"Gloria said that in many ways our life still will be 'un-normal,' so we should plug into as many normal things as we can—Sunday school, youth groups, and all the activities that will prevent a child from growing up lopsided. Anna will have the kinds of experiences all kids deserve." Obviously, Sandi has taken Gloria's advice to heart.

It was during 1984, when Sandi finally had a child of her own, that she began the Friendship Club for children. Geared for youngsters age fifteen and under, the club features newsletters, a calendar of activities and thoughts for each day, and notes from Sandi, as well as things to color and other activities. "Kids are exposed to so many negative things these days, and we want to get some positive, life-changing ideas inside their heads," she explained. "These things may not mean a whole lot to them right now, but maybe later on when they are faced with an important decision, they will be able to draw on some of the principles we have shared with them. We never know what kind of impact this will have on their lives."

But 1984 was not just a year of giving birth in Sandi's world. These words from Ecclesiastes—"There is a time for everything . . . a time to be born and a time to die"—must have been on Sandi's mind in July when two close relatives passed away.

Reverend Floyd Tunnell, Sandi's grandfather, died only a few months after Anna had been born. He had come back from Lindsay, California, and only been in Anderson a short while before his death. At the time of his death, Reverend Tunnell could see four generations—his four children, twelve grandchildren, and three great-grandchildren.

Reverend Tunnell was buried in the East Maplewood Cemetery on a slight incline, near a maple tree where friends and family sought shade on that July day. There are tall stately trees throughout the cemetery, giving the place a sense of peace and dignity.

Less than two weeks later, family and friends gathered together again in this same place to mourn the passing of Donald T. Tunnell, the oldest son of Reverend Tunnell. He was forty-eight years old when he died in Indianapolis, leaving behind three children, Sandi's cousins Tamra, Monica, and Donald Scott, who all live in Indianapolis.

Don Tunnell was buried beside his father. Their graves are marked by a single red granite marker.

30

Sandi continued to tour heavily to support a new album and began her From the Heart tour on September 6 in Wichita. It covered forty-three cities before finishing on December 11 in Fort Wayne, Indiana. Her appearance at the Praise Gathering in Indianapolis was before ten thousand people—the largest crowd ever—who came to celebrate the tenth anniversary of this event. Sandi served as hostess of the Friday evening concert, where she and Larnelle introduced their new duet, "I've Just Seen Jesus," to a live audience. Their performance received a standing ovation.

Just before the official tour began, Sandi performed with the Bill Gaither Trio in an afternoon grandstand concert at the Ohio State Fair, along with the New Gaither Vocal Band and Larnelle Harris. It was the first time a major Christian group had been featured at this fair, the largest in the United States; fifty thousand people watched the performance. In fact, the crowd was so large that officials had to close the grandstand an hour before the concert. Only Alabama drew more people for a single performance and only Willie Nelson drew more total people (for two performances). Gospel music was coming of age.

Sandi kept her ties with Anderson College during this tour, performing at the Homecoming Concert. She performed two concerts that evening, both before a packed house at Reardon Auditorium, but she could not stay in Anderson long—the Friday night concert was squeezed between one in Louisville the night before and one in Atlanta the night after.

The From the Heart tour was a major one for Sandi because it was her first solo tour. She had received major exposure with the Bill Gaither Trio and been the opening act for the Imperials, but she had never before attempted a solo tour where she would headline in major auditoriums and other secular venues. She was a little nervous about it, but knew the time had come to take the big step. Still, in the back of her mind, she couldn't help but wonder if people would actually show up and pay money to see just her.

She should not have spent a moment worrying because it was a huge success, with over three hundred thousand seeing her during the eighty-eight-day tour. The December 1 date in Memphis had been sold out since the end of October and the Anderson date had sold out in two days, prompting a second concert. Promoters also scheduled second concerts in Wheaton, Illinois; Houston, Texas; and Akron, Ohio, because of the huge demand for tickets.

Sandi said of her concerts, "I like to be myself at a concert—I hope that during an evening people experience many different emotions during the course of my concert—I hope they can laugh, be quiet and pensive, and I hope that something I sing touches their heart and maybe even causes them to shed a tear. I want people to go away from one of my concerts with a renewed commitment to the Lord and to their family."

Sandi appeared on the cover of *CCM* for the second time in the December 1984 issue. In an interview with Davin Seay, she said, "My growth as a solo artist has been mercifully very gradual. I really had no aspirations or dreams to be doing what I'm doing now." She explained, "We put together a little tour in California and it was around then [the time of her first album] that we began to realize it was more than just a part-time hobby. We told the Lord that if what He wanted was for us to get into music full-time, then we were ready. Not long afterward, Bill Gaither called and asked if I'd be interested in singing backup with them. It was a real confirmation."

Sandi was also aware of her audience and her place in gospel music, stating, "I know now who I'm singing for. My ministry is directed to the body of Christ. The assumption I make is that people already know about Jesus. But that doesn't mean that there still isn't hurt, or that marriages aren't falling apart, or that there might not be emotional, financial, or physical needs." This acceptance of herself and her ministry had taken a while for Sandi to accept, and she notes, "I used to feel that I had to do everything—to minister to people on the street and reach the unsaved. But here's where I belong. Maybe I don't participate directly in healing the body, but I believe that my music serves as an encouragement and, perhaps, will give others insight and a way to apply God's truth."

Sandi told *Virtue* magazine, "I've always wanted to be a communicator, and music is the avenue that I'm most comfortable with. I want to communicate in a way that people can understand. I think that is one of the things that Jesus has impressed upon my mind. He spent so much of His time going out to where the people were; He didn't wait for them to reach His level before He could communicate with them. If a man were a fisherman, He would go out and fish with him; and then talk to him."

Sandi told *Cash Box,* a secular music trade, "My music and voice are simply vessels to fulfill my purpose. Music is an extra—the means to an end. If I can take my audience and renew its joy and commitment to the Lord, I have fulfilled my purpose." But there was another side of Sandi, too, a side that was trying to cope with the emerging fame. She confessed, "In the beginning it was hard to pace myself. There were so many opportunities, so many places to be. And I began to lose sight of what it was I was doing."

But it was always her roots that gave her stability and she admitted, "Nothing is more stabilizing than family, having them close around you. Both John's parents and mine live in Anderson. So do all our brothers and sisters. Sometimes, out on the road, you have a tendency to think that it's reality—that everyone is supposed to wait on you and come to your beck and call. When I get home, the first thing Mom asks is how my concerts went, then she tells me to get in the kitchen and help with the dishes."

Sandi was also going through the stage many celebrities go through as they find themselves increasingly famous and perceived as "glamorous." "Other people see me only at concerts or on record covers. They may see me as a 'star,' " she said. "But I see myself at the times when I have no makeup on, when my hair is messed up, when I stumble out of bed in the middle of the night to check on Anna. I see myself as just a very 'normal' person."

There was one interesting new development in Sandi Patti's future plans, which she revealed in a late 1984 interview. "I'd really like to do a Christian variety show," she said. "Not syrupy or preachy, just good music. Mind you, I'm not going to do any of this tomorrow. The time and situation need to be right."

31

The election of 1984 was the high point for the Christian culture, which felt a unity as it gathered behind Ronald Reagan in his quest for a second term in the White House. At this point, the Christian culture was at its strongest and those in the movement were at their most influential, united by their belief in themselves and their Creator.

When Ronald Reagan captured 59 percent of the popular vote in the 1984 presidential election against Walter Mondale—capturing every state except Minnesota—Republicans and the religious right both looked at the outcome as a mandate for their ideas, views, and programs. For fundamentalists, especially, there was an overriding, overwhelming belief that they possessed insights the country needed to hear. Among those insights was an attack on "secular humanism," which became a euphemism for anything the fundamentalists were against.

These fundamentalists held demanding, rigid beliefs, traditional values, and an absolute certainty about things temporal and eternal. They promulgated absolutist moral teachings and had an infectious enthusiasm for evangelism.

In the 1984 election, the fundamentalists and righteous right proclaimed it loud and clear: "God is definitely a Republican." Their view of government was that it had become a moral evil infecting American society, so they took it upon themselves to create a new government, born from the will of God, that would bring America back to morality and make it an invulnerable fortress.

It has always been easier to unite the Republican party because it is more narrowly defined ideologically. The Democrats, in trying to represent minorities, outcasts, the poor, the disenfranchised, and others, have a much more difficult time presenting a united front: What appeals to one segment offends another and they are always in danger of alienating the main body of middle-class Americans with their suppport of fringe elements. In this election, political conservatives found themselves united with Christian fundamentalists, who found their faith compatible with the Republican party platform.

Thus the 1984 presidential election became a vote for or against Christianity and the Christian culture. Some statistics bear this out: It was discovered that those giving to conservative Political Action Committees (PACs) were the most religious, while those giving to liberal PACs were the least. Twenty percent of Democrats claimed no religious preference against only 6 percent of Republicans who held this view. White evangelical Protestants account for about 20 percent of the United States population and, as evangelical leaders pushed voter registration, the payoff came: 80 percent of white evangelicals voted for Reagan.

Coming out of this Republican Christian movement were several views of Jesus. One view held that "Jesus always goes first-class" and those who held this view found it easy to adopt the new commandment of the upwardly mobile in the mid-1980s: "Enrich thyself." For these poeple, Christians could not—would not—tolerate being second-class citizens in any way, shape, or form. God had created this world for them—His chosen ones—and it was His intention to give them all the desires of their heart and bless them abundantly in all ways with the very best.

Another concept that emerged is the warrior/God or military Jesus. This Jesus will smite those who oppose Him, but it is up to the Christian to make sure God's side is sufficiently armed. This concept is also tied to the notion that spiritual battles are constantly being waged with the forces of Heaven and Hell vying for nations as well as individual souls. This makes each Christian a spiritual soldier.

The final image of Jesus is one of an easygoing Jesus who is the eternal nice guy around Christians. They love Him, He loves them, and whatever they do is just fine because it's all in the family and the blood will bind all wounds. Sandi Patti has expressed this sentiment, saying, "Jesus and I have become real friends. He laughs with me, cries with me, rejoices with me, and even scolds me, as good friends ought to do. Jesus is on my side, He believes in me, He's pulling for me. With that kind of support, how can I go wrong?"

The positive side of this view is that it makes God personal—interested in the most menial and mundane aspects of a person's life. It is anthropomorphic, causing the believer to look at God (and Jesus) as some sort of Superman, basically human with supernatural powers. And, by humanizing God, the believer finds Him easier to relate to.

On the negative side, this can also trivialize God, so that the believer loses sight of the big picture and sees a limited God who picks at small details.

In the Christian culture in general, and contemporary Christian music in particular, these views of God emerged in sermons, books, and songs. The "Jesus always goes first-class" view was reflected in the affluent lifestyles and materialism of this group; the warrior/God was reflected in the flag-waving patriotism, pro-nuclear movement, and military buildup, as well as songs where a vengeful, angry God waged war on those against Him. The "Jesus is my best friend" theology could be heard on countless songs floating through the airwaves and through stereo speakers.

Music was becoming an increasingly dominant and important part of the Christian culture. The songs expressed the theology and views of this culture and the singers and musicians openly proclaimed their allegiance to these Christian-based philosophies. But there were still some reservations within this culture about some of the music from Christian musicians—particularly gospel rock. As music became as much a matter of style as content—and fashion became linked closely with the music—the traditionally conservative Christian culture often found it difficult to support musicians who wore the fashions of pop culture while singing their gospel songs.

In news from the world, 1984 is remembered as the year the Olympics came to Los Angeles and the United States put on a show to show the world what an extravaganza these games could be. At the Democratic Convention, the first woman vice presidental candidate, Geraldine Ferraro, was placed on the ballot and Bishop Desmond Tutu was named the recipient of the Nobel Peace Prize, focusing attention on the problems of South Africa.

In music it was the year of *Purple Rain* by Prince and the Revolution, *Private Dancer* by Tina Turner, *Like a Virgin* by Madonna, *Sports* by Huey Lewis and the News, *Valote* by Julian Lennon, *Lush Life* by Linda Ronstadt, and the album that rocked the rockers, *Born in the U.S.A.* by Bruce Springsteen.

32

"To be very honest, I was not looking forward to going at first because I'm gone so much. All I could think was, 'I have to be gone from home again,' " said Sandi about her trip to Israel in early 1985. But that reluctant attitude soon changed when she arrived in the Holy Land.

"It was a very spiritual experience for me to understand the Scriptures a little bit better," said Sandi. "To see the places which Jesus saw. And when you're out in the middle of the Sea of Galilee, and you look around the mountain and you see all these cities up on top of the hill that you can't miss because they're right there—to understand Jesus' words when He relates that to our life—that a city on a hill *cannot* be hid, and to be in that setting where He probably got that inspiration from, as *He* looked around and saw that."

Sandi had clearly been moved by the experience and she could not hold back her excitement. "There's this gigantic rock, and up on top of the rock was a shrine to the god Pan," she said, "and also what they think was Herod's summer home—built up on this rock. And Jesus with His Disciples in Caesarea Philippi, was in that setting, looking up at the shrine for the god of Pan, and Herod's home, and saying to His Disciples, 'Who do others say that I am?' And then He asked Peter, 'Who do *you* say that I am?' Peter said, 'You are the Christ, the Son of God.' He says, 'Peter, upon *that* rock—not upon *this* rock—but upon *that* rock, that solid foundation, that understanding, I will build my Kingdom.' And, I tell you, that really came alive to me. To see that whole thing. That's what Jesus did—He used what was there to make a very eternal point."

All of the experiences in Israel moved Sandi deeply, but the one that had the most profound impact was the garden tomb. It was the high point of the trip for Sandi because, she said, "As I sat there . . . I thought, 'It is because of this place, because all that has happened here, that's why I do what I do! That's why my life has meaning. It's because Jesus Christ is alive!' And to have them explain to you all the factual things that prove that He couldn't possibly have been stolen, His body been stolen, to see the validity of the Scriptures, from people who were Christians, and those who were not even Christians, to know not just by faith, but to know also by the facts and the truth that Jesus Christ is alive."

Sandi could not stop words from pouring forth. "He is why I want to sing—that the whole world may know that He is alive." And with that, she stopped talking and sat back, her eyes still intense, her gestures still animated.

The trip had been planned and organized by Bill and Gloria Gaither, who had been to Israel several years before, loved it, and wanted to return. They searched for a way to take something back to the Israeli people because they felt they had been given so much. Finally they came up with the idea of doing some concerts there as well as touring the Holy Land and soaking up their heritage. They asked Sandi and John to be a part of this and the Helverings quickly said yes out of friendship and respect—although Sandi admitted later that, at the time, she would rather have spent the winter days at her home in Anderson as the time approached to leave.

The visible result of the Holy Land trip, for Sandi Patti fans and followers, was a twenty-one-minute documentary video directed by Robert Deaton and produced by David Crabtree for Mizpah Communications, Inc. In this video, Sandi and Larnelle Harris each reflect on what they are seeing during their Israel trip and how it is affecting them. In the documentary, they are shown shopping in the ancient, crowded marketplace in Jerusalem, singing a hymn on a boat sailing the Sea of Galilee, standing at the barbed-wired Israeli-Lebanon border, and visiting several other famous landmarks where Jesus lived and taught.

Sandi sings "Via Dolorosa" as she walks down the Via Dolorosa and Sandi and Larnelle perform "I've Just Seen Jesus," a Resurrection song about finding the empty tomb where Jesus' body had been laid. This was released on Larnelle's album of that same title.

After the filming in January (done by a special video team of American and Israeli filmmakers) the footage was brought back to the States and edited, then released for sale in May. Additionally, the song segments—"Via Dolorosa" and "I've Just Seen Jesus"—were made available to television stations for airing.

Also in January came the announcement that two of Sandi's albums—*Songs from the Heart* and *Live . . . More Than Wonderful*—would be released by Benson on compact discs. The CD market had been growing since the introduction of compact disc players to the marketplace a couple of years before. The first releases were primarily classical music albums (to take advantage of the affluent buyers and number of audiophiles in that market), but the rest of the musical world was following quickly. Unfortunately, there were a limited number of CD manufacturing plants (only one in the United States) and the backlog created a major problem with gospel music because gospel labels were put on the back burner. So Benson's plan to release CDs was thwarted temporarily.

When the Grammy nominees were announced in January 1985, Sandi Patti's album *Songs from the Heart* was nominated in the Best Gospel Performance, Female, category, along with Amy Grant, who won the award for her song "Angels Watching Over Me." Of the thirty-five nominations in the gospel categories, only two came from major secular labels—the Christian labels controlled thirty-three of the nominations.

The sixteenth annual Dove Awards once again made the statement that the gospel world does not care what the pop world thinks

—it is going to honor the artists who appeal most directly to the Christian audience. And that meant that Sandi Patti collected three Doves—including Female Vocalist for the fourth consecutive year, Inspirational Album for her *Songs from the Heart* LP, and the top honor, Artist of the Year.

Accepting the awards, Sandi said, "I've learned a lot this year, I've learned so much from the Lord. To obey His wishes is my heart's desire." Accepting the Female Vocalist award, she said, "I know that God's grace is sufficient." Backstage Sandi elaborated: "It's never just one more award. Every year is something special." Sandi also announced that she was going to give one of her Dove trophies to her daughter, "who has made me a better person." She also sent words of thanks to the "Bible Study Fellowship ladies back home."

Sandi performed "Upon This Rock," written by Gloria Gaither and Dony McGuire, which later received the Dove for Song of the Year. Amy Grant received the Dove for Contemporary Album for her *Straight Ahead* LP.

In spring 1985 the hottest song out was "We Are the World" by U.S.A. for Africa, a group of rock stars that included Lionel Richie, Paul Simon, Ray Charles, Bob Dylan, Kenny Rogers, Bruce Springsteen, Cyndi Lauper, Michael Jackson, Diana Ross, and others with producer Quincy Jones, who had gotten together to record the song to aid victims of the Ethiopian disaster. After the Dove Awards, a number of Christian artists went over to a Nashville studio to do their version of that event. Organized by Steve Camp and called CAUSE (Christian Artists United to Save the Earth), the song they performed and released was "Do Something Now."

Those performing solos on the song were Amy Grant, Larry Norman, Kathy Troccoli, Evie Karlsson, Phil Keaggy, Scott Wesley Brown, Michele Pillar, Steve Camp, Russ Taff, Dana Key, Mylon LeFevre, Jessy Dixon, Steve Taylor, Matthew Ward, 2nd Chapter of Acts, Sheila Walsh, and Sandi Patti. Those singing on the chorus included Shirley Caesar, Gary Chapman, the Bill Gaither Trio, Steve Green, Lisa Whelchel, Doug Oldham, Silverwind, Glenn

Kaiser, Lanny Wolfe, Pam Mark Hall, Ed DeGarmo, Chris Christian, Bobby Jones and New Life, Glad, Sherman Andrus, Bob Farrell, Found Free, Rick Cua, and others. It was released in May on seven-inch and twelve-inch singles and cassettes (with artist interviews) to Christian radio stations and bookstores. A fifteen-minute video, which included conversations with the artists, was also made available.

The idea originally came from singer/songwriter Steve Camp while he was watching the video of "Do They Know It's Christmas?" by Band Aid, a group of British singers organized by Bob Geldof. Camp called several artists, asking if they would take part in a project to raise money to fight world hunger. They all gave positive responses. Camp also called Billy Ray Hearn, president of Sparrow Records, and he gave his total support of the project, which would be released on that label.

Originally, Camp wanted to have the song recorded and released in January, but conflicts in schedules did not permit any significant number of top gospel artists to gather together at one time. So then Camp revised his plan and decided on a session during GMA Week when most would be in town.

The title of the song came from a talk given by noted Christian author and speaker Anthony Campolo. Camp and Campolo had shared a concert stage in Denver at the end of February and Camp, impressed with Campolo's theme, "Do something now," picked it up and wrote a rough draft of the song. Camp then met with songwriter Phil Madeira in March. Madeira had also been working on a song about world hunger and they got together with Rob and Carol Frazier and the songs were combined and polished: The result was the final version of "Do Something Now." On March 11 they recorded a demo.

A letter was sent out to Christian musicians and singers by mid-March to encourage them to take part in the project; at GMA Week, each singer's registration packet had a rehearsal and recording schedule, cassette tape of "Do Something Now" with instrumental tracks and scratch vocal, lead sheets of the song, release forms, and information on Compassion International, the relief organization that would receive the income from the song. All the musicians and studios donated their time.

Sandi's line in "Do Something Now" comes after the first chorus. When Sandi came in and initially put her part down, the first take sounded very "traditional." Camp encouraged her to get more gritty and Sandi, her years as a studio singer paying off, let it all out and finished her part in ten minutes—perfect and true to the song.

The big group chorus was taped after the Doves had concluded. Before midnight, when the singers were scheduled to arrive, Ed Query put the finishing touches on the CAUSE banner that acted as a backdrop for the group; studio hands arranged the riser where the chorus stood.

A few minutes past midnight, the studio was full of Christian artists, musicians, executives, and news media representatives. Coordinator Steve Wyer stood before the chorus and introduced Camp, who led the group in prayer, then a hymn rose from the singers: "He Is Lord." John Fischer—who confessed, "We're late again, but it's good for us to be humbled"—concerning the fact that rock artists did this first—publically thanked Bob Geldof and admitted: "Recording a group song for the needy isn't an original idea, but it's a good one for borrowing." Then he passed out communion—three loaves of bread and three large cups of grape juice. He read from 1 Corinthians 11: "Therefore, whoever eats the bread or drinks the cup of the Lord in an unworthy manner will be guilty of sinning against the body and blood of the Lord. A man ought to examine himself before he eats of the bread and drinks of the cup. For anyone who eats and drinks without recognizing the body of the Lord eats and drinks judgment on himself." Then Mylon LeFevre prayed over the bread and Bill Gaither prayed over the cup.

Wes Stafford, assistant to the president of Compassion International, spoke to the group and thanked the artists for donating their time before saying that 100 percent of the funds received by the relief organization from the sale of records and associated merchandising would go to aid in Africa, adding, "We're not going to hold anything back for overhead." He explained further that the funds would go primarily for food and medical supplies and the infrastructure to transport the supplies, with Compassion working in conjunction with the Sudan Interior Mission. This group has been working in Africa for almost ninety years and in Ethiopia for fifty years.

A film crew scurried about as Cam Floria directed the singers on the chorus. On the front row was Evie, Amy Grant, Sandi, Gary Chapman, Russ Taff, Steve Camp, Sheila Walsh, Larry Norman, Michele Pillar, and Jessy Dixon and just in front of them were the children who sang on the song earlier in the day. During a brief lull, the whole group spontaneously broke into "We Will Stand," a song composed by Russ and Tori Taff.

By 3 A.M. the singalong session was finished, press photos had been taken, and the singers were milling around in the hallway, signing the group poster. The film crew was about to begin shooting the soloists doing their lines while some left to go home. But most could not go home, could not pull themselves away, and even a little after 5 A.M. there were still about a dozen people in the studio. Finally, just before 6 A.M., Steve Camp led another prayer, saying, "Lord, we're so weak . . . but You are strong. Without You we can do nothing. You've brought this together. Take this small offering, this meal, these few loaves of bread in our lunch pail, and multiply it for Your glory." And so the session ended, bringing to a close perhaps contemporary Christian music's finest moment.

33

In the spring of 1985, during a time when a number of concerts had been scheduled, a major crisis came into Sandi's life. Anna was hospitalized after a severe reaction to some medication. Sandi and John flew back home after each concert to be with Anna at the hospital. This crisis reflected a maturing of Sandi as an artist and minister and a realization of the work she does. The decision to honor the concert commitments, Sandi said, "was not choosing my career over my daughter. That had nothing to do with it. It was choosing to be faithful to the Lord." She added, "Sometimes that has meant canceling my concerts and staying home."

Anna's sickness happened just before her first birthday and Sandi admits the three weeks spent in the hospital were "a horrible time for us." But she also saw it as "a growing time. When we go through something like that we have a choice—we can endure it or we can go through it triumphantly. There were days when I would cry all day and think, 'Lord, why is this happening to us? I just don't understand.' And there were days when I would say, 'O.K., Lord, I don't understand, but I am choosing to trust You.' That's all we can do. I don't know how people can go through a crisis without the Lord. I honestly don't know."

Sandi had come to a new awareness regarding her role as a Christian singer after studying the book of Romans with her Bible Study Fellowship group. "Before I studied the book of Romans, I had always started with my feelings and tried to fit the facts with my feelings," she admitted. "But now I've learned to start with the facts, and let my feelings and actions come from the facts."

Sandi states she has learned there are "four things a Christian should do in times of crisis. The first thing is to continue to acknowledge that God is in control . . . [secondly] to make sure your physical needs are being met. Thirdly, we should not do something rash or unnecessary out of panic and, fourth, we must assess the situation correctly." With Anna's sickness, Sandi realized that her parents and John's parents were there to look after Anna and that the child "was asleep 99 percent of the time and she didn't know if we were there or not." Still, Sandi added, "That didn't mean that every time I walked out of the hospital my heart wasn't breaking. But there is a peace that keeps our hearts and minds set, not in our problems, but in Christ Jesus."

The growing awareness and realization of her role as a Christian singer began to come to Sandi in 1984. She told *Charisma,* "I have always known that I am singing because I have been called to it by the Lord. But I had never known exactly *why.* But as I was studying the life of Paul, I began to see that he had such a purpose in his life and that he knew why he was doing it. So I really prayed that the Lord would show me why I was singing."

Sandi is involved in a Bible Study Fellowship group with some other ladies in her hometown of Anderson. BSF is an interdenominational religious organization consisting of individual Bible study groups meeting weekly around the world. This course stresses daily, personal Bible study through questions for individual study, discussion groups for sharing insights, lectures with practical applications, and written summary notes. The organization is based in San Antonio, Texas. Sandi's group prays for her and her concerts—including the people who will be coming to the concerts. When Sandi goes on the road, it is usually for two weeks at a time—the tour usually leaves on a Wednesday night, is gone the next week, and then returns the following Tuesday night. Since her BSF group meets on Wednesday mornings, Sandi attends often. Also, she takes the lessons with her on the road and does them daily, often posting the home discussion questions on the bus to discuss during the traveling time.

During the time Sandi was praying about learning "why" she was singing, the BSF group was studying Romans. Sandi, relating her experience, begins by paraphrasing the beginning of Romans, saying, " 'Paul, called to be a disciple, set apart for the Gospel of Christ . . .' We are called to be Christians and we are called to be disciples. Some of us are set apart in the accounting field, some in the counseling field, some in the gospel field. I knew I was set apart in the gospel field."

She continued, "Then in verses 12–15 Paul says, talking about the church, 'I long to see you, to encourage you . . .' That spoke to me. The Bible also says to be encouraged by one another's faith. So what I am doing is encouraging my brothers and sisters in the faith. I used to feel that if I was not ministering to non-Christians, then I wasn't doing any good. But there is so much hurt among Christians, so many decisions to make, and so much influence of the world, the church needs to be encouraged. So I understood *why* I was singing for the first time."

The Bible Study Fellowship group answered another prayer for Sandi by giving her a trusted friend—Bev Grady—she could confide in and share her deepest thoughts with. Sandi admits she had reached "a very dry point in my walk with the Lord. I was expending so much emotional and spiritual energy in concerts and I was not—at my choice, as I look back on it—choosing to 'tank up.' " So she began to pray "about having somebody in my life I could tell absolutely anything to, because sometimes as a performer you feel you aren't given the luxury of 'down times.' Or, if you are, it has to be accompanied by a great deal of explanation.

"I prayed for somebody who understood music and understood the stress of travel," Sandi said. "It was at that time I began Bible Study Fellowship and met Bev. She has meant a great deal to me. Her faith and trust in the Lord and her willingness to give of herself are beautiful. She's been an answer to prayer for me."

By the end of 1985, Sandi Patti could safely say she had achieved "celebrity" status because *People* magazine, the chronicle of celebrities, covered her. In this major article, Sandi said, "I don't tell people, 'You have to believe this,' but rather, 'Hey, the things that Jesus taught and continues to teach flat-out work, and this is where I've been and learned and maybe it fits where you're at right now.' Music is a powerful tool. We should use it to help shape positive values."

Sandi said of her husband, "I honestly don't think I would have done this without John. Success for me doesn't depend on charts and dollars and cents. I'll know I've made it if I have a happy husband, and if my child grows up loving us and loving the Lord. The verdict's out on all those." Then she paused a moment before laughing and adding, "Well, not on my husband."

Sandi admitted that a number of people had told her she should "cross over" so more people could hear her. But she countered that argument, stating, "I think that we have all been called to share the Gospel in different ways. There are people whose music is more readily acceptable to the mainstream, who are called to share with people who aren't necessarily Christians, and we should support those people in our prayers. But for myself, right now, I feel very strongly that my ministry should be directed to people who are already familiar with the Christian way of life."

As Sandi became more successful, more journalists unfamiliar with her career interviewed her and asked her about her beginnings, which allowed her to reflect on the start of her career from the perspective of a successful award-winning performer. In one interview, she said about her early career: "It wasn't that I was unwilling to go out and perform. But I had seen so many people have problems because they misread what God had called them to do. I know [Christian] singers who have quit their jobs and taken their families out on the road because they felt 'called' to do so and it's been really hard for them. I wanted to be sure that God was really calling me to do this rather than it being something that I was trying to push myself into and telling myself that it was God's will when it really was *my* will. So my husband John and I took our time about deciding to go out on the road."

At another time she said, "The priorities of my life have always been clearly defined, and as I get older, they are becoming even more so. The Lord has always been the most important One to me, my family has been second, and my career has been third. Just because your career is down there in third place doesn't mean it's not important. It's just that there are other things that take precedence over it."

Sandi also reflected on the toll fame and the limelight takes on her spiritual life. She admitted, "About three years ago I woke up one day and realized, 'This is very unbalanced here.' It just shook me, in a way that really made me more serious about committing every area of my life—my family, my career, everything—to God. I had not really done that from my heart before. In my head I had, but I had not made that total commitment from my heart.

"It was a hard time for me. There were some things I had to work through, and I had to be honest with the people around me. Through all of it, God was very faithful and gave me forgiveness. That is a wonderful and exciting thing, to know we are forgiven and that we can start anew. I said, 'Lord, here are my failings, too.' You know, the Lord doesn't want anything less than what we are. Or anything more than what we are. And if we sometimes fail, He wants us to give Him that. So I learned not to wait until I am perfect, because then He would not be able to help me. He wants me as I am right now."

Sandi told *Charisma:* "My heart's desire is to be a disciple of Jesus Christ and that doesn't come from doing concerts or albums or anything else. It comes from John 8:31–32: 'If you continue in My Word, you will truly be My disciple and you will know the truth.' That is my heart's desire. As I continue to study God's Word. I realize I am placed in a position to be listened to, whether in a concert or on an album. I have to be sure that the things I say are rooted in the words of my Father. There are kids and young adults who listen to what I say. I pray that I can guide them to find out about what the Father has to say."

She concludes, "And, as we become disciples and children of God daily, we are able to see other Christians not from our perspective, but from God's perspective, and are able to say, 'You know what? They're learning too.' Then, rather than being so critical of each other, we should be praying about the matter—that God will show them, or maybe that God will show me.

"I would like to see more unity in the body of Christ. We need each other an awful lot. That doesn't mean we have to agree on everything, but . . . the only 'Jesus' that a lot of people are going to see is how we respond to our brothers and sisters."

34

Just before the CAUSE sessions, Cam Floria, director and founder of the Continental Singers and the Christian Artists Seminars in the Rockies, Europe, and Asia, had put together an album to raise money to feed the hungry. On that album, Sandi sang a heart-stopping number, "No Other Name."

Sandi was involved in another plea to help alleviate world hunger in 1985. In her *Songs from the Heart* album sleeve, there was a small message encouraging others to support World Vision, a Christian relief organization that Sandi personally endorsed.

Sandi also sang a song, "The Door Is Open," for the soundtrack to the movie, *Papa Was a Preacher,* released in 1985. The movie stars Robert Pine, Georgia Engel, Dean Stockwell, and Imogene Coca and the soundtrack was released on Word.

In 1985 Sandi Patti ended her affiliation with the Benson Company, a partnership that began in 1979 with the *Love Overflowing* album. The Helverings were involved in renegotiating Sandi's contract during a time when there was a great deal of change and reshuffling at the label. The split came primarily from Zondervan's and Benson's attempts to restructure their operation while their top-selling artist was looking for a safe, secure recording situation.

Sandi has noted that the spring and summer were frustrating times in their relationship with Benson. "We had spent months working on this, and just when we were able to agree on some things and everybody was happy, another change took place," said Sandi. "And John and I thought, 'Lord, are You trying to tell us that we should get out of this?' "

To frustrate matters even more, Anna was in the hospital. Still, Sandi found the strength to continue. "If we had not understood why we were in this business, we might have considered getting out altogether," she states. "But because we had learned back in February that our purpose was encouragement, we knew not to change our direction drastically." Finally, after months of tiring negotiations, "We just thought maybe it was time for us to make some changes regarding the record company," said Sandi.

The Benson Company had been founded in 1902 by John T. Benson, his wife Eva, and Reverend J. O. McClurkan as a publishing company, distributing religious pamphlets in the Nashville area. In 1904 the Benson Company published its first songbook, *Living Water Songs,* but it remained a very small local company until 1935 when John T. Benson, Jr., took over. The business grew from grossing $12,000 a year to an annual gross of $100,000 a year betweeen 1948 and 1951.

Bob Benson, second son of John T. Jr. and the third generation of Bensons involved with the company, joined the organization in 1960 and soon the company's revenues were over the half-million-dollar mark. The company made its first foray into the recording industry with the formation of HeartWarming Records. John T. Benson III joined the organization in 1969 after the company had been successful with its first artists, which included the Speer Family, the Rambos, and the Bill Gaither Trio, and the company expanded into contemporary Christian music in the 1970s, away from the Southern gospel quartet sound they had begun with.

The company has remained in Nashville since its founding but was sold in 1980 to the Zondervan Corporation, a Christian publishing firm based in Grand Rapids, Michigan, known best for publishing Bibles and its chain of Family Bookstores located in a number of shopping malls. The sale came after Bob Benson stepped down from the presidency to devote his life to speaking and ministry (he had learned he had terminal cancer) and John T. Benson III decided to retire.

The company, which encompasses a number of labels, including HeartWarming, Impact, Power Disc, and Greentree, as well as a large music publishing operation, underwent a major restructuring in July 1985. The Benson Company had announced that Sandi had re-signed with them in July in the midst of this upheaval, but the agreement was only for her *Hymns* album. There would be no long-term contract or commitment from the Helverings. Ironically, this announcement came only a short time after the RIAA had notified Sandi and the Benson Company that her *Live . . . More Than Wonderful* album had achieved gold status, signifying sales of over half a million units. To celebrate this event, the Benson Company honored Sandi with a special reception—attended by guests such as Deniece Williams and former Olympic ice skating champion Dorothy Hamill—and handed out gold albums to her and her creative team.

Benson was considered by the Helverings to be the "distributor" for Sandi's albums, while the Helverings kept control of the creative aspect through their own production company. They had learned early the essential role of a record label—to manufacture, promote, and distribute records—and kept creative control in their own corner. The record label traditionally likes to have a say in what goes on a record—the songs and type of music—because they have a knowledge of the marketplace and are aware of trends and gaps in the market. Unfortunately, their idea for what an artist should do and what the artist feels he or she should do are often at odds. However, since many artists don't have a clear idea of the musical direction they should take, the company is allowed to dictate musical direction. A major disadvantage here is that this often leads to derivative music or "corporate pop" because the label bases its decisions on what is already successful in the marketplace instead of attempting to create a new market with a fresh artistic vision. But a lot of artists, attempting to stay in good graces with the label and without the clout that comes from successful sales, fall prey to the label dictating their musical direction.

Sandi Patti *knows* what she should sing—music for the church—and knows which songs and material work best for her, so she needs—and wants—less input from the label. For the Helverings, a record label should market and distribute their product; therefore, the Helverings control the musical portion with their own production company and retain control over other creative aspects, such as song selection and the covers of the albums.

Originally entitled *Just for You . . . Twenty-two of Your Favorite Hymns,* the album *Hymns Just for You* was recorded at the Pinebrook Studio in Anderson. On the disc label for this album it says "Produced by Helvering Productions" prominently under "Benson." The copyright on the back states that the material is owned by Helvering Productions—not the Benson Company. This is a major step in the Helverings' business dealings with their record label and means that the *Hymns* album is owned by them and they can take it and re-release it on another label (or their own) at the end of a specified amount of time. It is also only a small step away from them having their own record label, keeping total control of Sandi's product (and anyone else's they chose to sign), and thus increasing their share of an album's profits.

The album reflects Sandi's love of these old songs and in the liner notes she says, "Time and time again I go back to the songs my grandparents sang with all their hearts, back to the songs I have been singing since I was a little girl, back to the simple yet life-changing truths that renew and refresh my spirit." During her concerts, questionnaires had been passed out asking audiences to mark their favorite hymns (from a list supplied) and the final selection was partially drawn from these responses—Sandi wanted to be sure the songs she chose reflected the tastes of her audience. Also, it was a good way to "test market" the product, knowing which songs her buying public liked and wanted to hear and then supplying them with these songs.

The album begins with "It Is Well With My Soul" and this

song, with its lush instrumentation and large orchestration, sets the stage for the rest of the album. Musically, the selections emphasize the drama the church desires, while lyrically, the songs express the traditional Christianity of the American church.

The album states that the medleys on the album were "realized" by Sandi, who found the message and music could flow together. These medleys work to Sandi's advantage because she is not burdened by having to do separate and distinct arrangements of each song and fight the obvious problem of having them sound so similar, as well as a marketing problem—how to include twenty-two songs and not have to do a double album, which would raise the retail price and make it harder to sell. Here, she has done one album that features a number of great songs and, by "realizing" medleys, has been able to combine the orchestration with high church drama and come up with an attractive package for listeners and buyers.

The front of the album features a picture of Sandi in a church pew, while the back shows John, Sandi, and Anna in a front pew, holding hymnals (with Sandi looking lovingly at Anna as the rest of the congregation sings). Behind her are her parents singing and in the third row is her grandmother Mable Tunnell. It is a very attractive cover for a very attractive album that lets Sandi touch her roots and affirm who she is—a singer for the church—as she presents to her audience the songs, drama, and orchestrated choral sound they love so much. In many ways this album was inevitable in Sandi's career, but the strength is that it came when she was secure with herself as a church singer, confident she was following the right musical path. Christian bookstore buyers agreed—there were 218,000 copies of the album presold before it was even released.

Sandi continued to tour throughout the 1985 year and appeared at key events such as Estes Park and the Christian Booksellers' Association Convention. In the fall, she appeared with the Bill Gaither Trio in seven cities during their Fully Alive tour.

Sandi's parents had moved back to Anderson from San Diego and were also traveling regularly to their own concerts and evange-

Performing in Nashville.

Sandi belts out a song with First Call's Bonnie Keen, Marty McCall, and Melody Tunney.

With hosts Pat Boone and Cheryl Prewitt during the 1985 Dove Awards. (CENTER FOR POPULAR MUSIC)

The home of John, Sandi, and Anna just east of Anderson in a suburban development.

In concert with "her kids" in Chattanooga.

Ron and Carolyn Patty with granddaughter Anna during a TV interview after the 1987 Dove Awards.

The Helverings—John, Anna, and Sandi—in a family pose after the 1987 Dove Awards.

Melody and Dick Tunney, winners of the 1987 Dove for Songwriters of the Year and writers of "Let There Be Praise," "I've Just Seen Jesus," "O Magnify the Lord," and other big hits for Sandi.

Sandi swept the 1987 Dove Awards, winning both Female Vocalist of the Year and Artist of the Year.

Truett Cathy, founder and president of Chick-fil-A, Inc., greets Sandi at the Atlanta-based headquarters. Chick-fil-A is the national sponsor of the 1987 Gospel Music Week and the Gospel Music Dove Awards Celebration. The company also sponsors Sandi's concert tours.

Sandi, after she signed with Word.

listic crusades. At Anderson College Sandi kept her ties, joining with other distinguished alumni in visiting Richard DeVos, president of Amway, during his campus visit.

Sandi began the 1985 year with *Songs from the Heart* at the top of the album sales chart, followed by *Live . . . More Than Wonderful* at number six. These two albums stayed on the charts all year (generally in the top ten), competing with Amy Grant's *Straight Ahead* and *Age to Age* albums. Amy Grant's *unguarded* album entered the charts at number one in August, the third consecutive album of hers to achieve this feat.

35

Philosopher Thomas Huxley once summed up Christianity as "being nice." While some theologians and fundamentalists might object vehemently to that assessment, the truth remains that it seems to be an inherent trait of the Christian culture. Most contemporary Christian musicians and singers grew up in nice Christian homes, comfortably middle class, and have grown into nice young parents with the same middle-class values. Their idea of being radical is playing gospel pop instead of the old hymns. Still, they remain, at heart, "good kids."

This niceness is reflected in the music and at the halfway mark in the 1980s a look at contemporary Christian music revealed that musically it was derivative and lyrically it was didactic. It sounded just like what was on the pop charts a year before, while, lyrically, it still sought to teach others what to believe, how to live, and why they should be Christians.

This niceness implies a code of behavior and, in many ways, the Christian church world is like a small town. What people think of you is important; you must be careful not to offend. Above all, you must never give the *appearance* of impropriety. The reasoning is that even if you are doing no wrong yourself, you could cause someone else to go astray.

If there is one word to describe Sandi and John's approach to her career it is "careful." They are always concerned they are making the right moves that will not offend anyone or be misconstrued so that the church world will not be alienated or offended.

Within the contemporary Christian music world, Sandi Patti is envied but not really respected by a number of other Christian singers and musicians. She is envied because of her success: large concert tours, major awards, gold records hanging on the wall, and so on. But she is not genuinely respected by a number within this world because her music is directed at the church audience, and she caters to this audience. This means that she does not challenge her audiences musically. She does not try to be an "artist," but is content to be a singer who delivers a message that her audience already believes, accepts, and wants to hear repeated. Since Sandi does not pursue "real art" (according to this crowd), she presents a music that is bland and boring to an audience that can be described the same way.

There are disparaging remarks heard about "Sandi Fatty" and some openly wonder how Sandi—not a raving beauty in the classic sense—could be so appealing to this audience. But she is and there is even a sex appeal here, especially among men who like a maternal figure or those who find the slim, willowy types unattractive. And there are also some who speak out against John Helvering. Why does Sandi give him so much of the credit for her success when it is her talent that has done it? These same people point out John's inadequacies as a manager and many tell stories of him overreacting emotionally in tough situations. But these people fail to see John and Sandi as a team. She needs him on the front line so she can devote herself to singing and developing herself spiritually. Also, they trust each other—he trusts her talent and she trusts his business decisions—so they allow each other to function in their own spheres of influence without a lot of second-guessing. It is a rare freedom and both benefit from it.

John and Sandi surmount their critics by being in tune with their audience—the church world—and presenting them with highly orchestrated, intensely emotional dramatic works in an attractive high-quality package. And they do this on a consistent basis.

John and Sandi have also developed an effective organization to promote Sandi's career and keep it moving forward. Their base is in Anderson—which keeps the small town flavor and appeal—but they use computers and good public relations to keep friends close, fans happy, and foes at bay. They manage to surround themselves with like-minded people with like-minded goals and ideals (mainly through hiring Anderson College students and graduates) to maintain a consistency in their professional organization.

These are all good reasons for Sandi's continued success as an act. But she has also been the beneficiary of the rise in popularity and acceptance of gospel music in the past twenty years, coming along at a fortuitous time for a Christian artist.

In music, 1985 was the year of Live Aid, the most widely seen and heard concert in the history of the world, as well as the Bruce Springsteen tour, which elevated him from rock star to cultural icon. The rock world learned to care and share as compassion came into fashion and celebrities began to see themselves in light of having a social responsibility and needing a social awareness. Indeed, it looked as if music might change the world for the better.

36

The year 1986 began with the tragedy of the space shuttle *Challenger.* Millions of Americans witnessed the deaths of the seven astronauts, including teacher Christa McAuliffe, on January 28. Two and a half weeks later, there was a tragedy much closer to Sandi and her family. Her brother Craig was involved in a near-fatal automobile wreck.

The accident occurred while a thick blanket of fog covered the area. It happened when his car rammed into the end of a semi near where two county roads come out on the main route, northwest of Anderson.

The accident was one of ten that occurred in the fog within a ten-minute period. It began with a small property damage accident and quickly turned into a chain reaction as approaching drivers were unable to stop in time, resulting in a number of rear-end collisions. Craig Patty, the last in line, incurred serious head injuries and was pinned in his vehicle for several minutes before the Pipe Creek Township fire fighters could free him. He was then taken to Mercy Hospital in Elwood and later flown on a Lifeline helicopter to Methodist Hospital in Indianapolis. Originally listed in critical condition, he was quickly put into the neuro constant care ward, where he remained in serious condition for several weeks.

For Sandi—and the entire Patty family—it was a time of deep

concern and fervent prayers as Craig fought for his life. Sandi spent as much time as possible with him at the hospital.

About a week after the accident, Sandi won a Grammy with Larnelle Harris in the Gospel Vocal, Duo or Group, category for "I've Just Seen Jesus." Amy Grant picked up her fourth consecutive Grammy for Gospel Vocal, Female, although Sandi had also been nominated in that category for her *Hymns Just for You* album.

At the 1986 Doves, a major upset occurred—Amy Grant won the Artist of the Year honors, temporarily ending Sandi's reign there. Amy bounded across the stage when the award was announced—but the stage was in Columbus, Ohio, at a sold-out concert. Not expecting to win, Amy and her management team had decided to avoid the GMA and continued doing concerts on her tour during the Dove festivities. They were stunned by the announcement.

Sandi again captured the Female Vocalist award—for the fifth consecutive time—but when asked backstage by a reporter whether she owned the award, she replied, "Oh no. There are so many talented people." "Via Dolorosa," a song that Sandi popularized, captured Song of the Year honors for its writers, Niles Borup and Billy Sprague. The show featured a rousing performance by Sandi and Larnelle doing "I've Just Seen Jesus."

Sandi had signed her contract with Word in Waco, Texas, in front of the entire Word music and record sales, marketing, and international distribution staff. The contract was described as a "multi-record marketing and distribution" agreement and Word was clearly excited. The largest gospel label, accounting for about 70 to 80 percent of the gospel music product sold in this country, now had their competitor's top seller.

Word was begun in the fall of 1950 by Jarrell McCracken, a Baylor student, who had recorded a spoken word allegory of a football game and Christianity. This recording of "The Game of Life" provided the beginning of an organization that would eventually call itself a "Christian communications company" and dominate gospel music.

After this first venture, McCracken—who was working his way through Baylor as a sports announcer—began recording singing artists, beginning with Frank Boggs in 1951. The company struggled through its first few years and in 1954 entered the wholesale distribution business for records, distributing jazz, classical, and children's records in addition to their own product. They were out of this business by 1957, but had started the Family Record Club by then and began to learn about direct mail.

In 1960 Word purchased Sacred Records, a label owned by Ralph Carmichael. At that time, Word was selling $4 million worth of records annually. The acquisition allowed Word to enter the music publishing business and in 1965 they began a book publishing division.

Word began other record labels under its umbrella to handle various kinds of music—Canaan for Southern gospel, Myrrh for contemporary Christian—and had learned a valuable lesson with their distributing operation. Beginning in 1960, Word sold directly to record outlets and Christian bookstores instead of having their product serviced by wholesale distribution companies. This allowed the company to effectively promote their own product and offer special price incentives.

In 1976 Word was purchased by ABC Entertainment Corporation, owners of the ABC television network. When ABC Records, another division of this company, was sold to MCA in 1979, Word remained at ABC under the corporate umbrella. However, in March 1986, ABC merged with Capital Cities, Inc., and the new organization wanted a stronger say in the running of the company. In September 1986, Jarrell McCracken left Word after thirty-five years at the helm and another executive was promoted from within to run the company. By this time, Word had an $80 million annual income.

Morning Like This was released by Word in February in record, cassette tape, and compact disc versions simultaneously worldwide. They also provided special merchandising stands to Christian bookstores that allowed all three configurations to be displayed, as well as ten Studio Trax cassettes (accompaniment tapes for each of the songs) and the *Morning Like This* songbook.

This release is Sandi's most mature album, lyrically and musically, in her career to date. It shows a depth and complexity her other albums had only hinted at. Here, her musical ideas have finally been developed on every song on the album and the lyrics express more than just praise or acknowledgment of God. Somehow Sandi manages to provide an album as stunning as her concerts, with a full range of feelings and emotions, that transcends American Christianity and elevates her beliefs to a more universal Christianity. It is a stunning achievement.

The album begins with "Let There Be Praise," a song with a long choral opening and distinctively Christian lyric, akin to her past albums. It is a bright up-tempo number and one begins to realize a key to Sandi's praise songs is that she manages to wed contemporary technology, dramatic intensity in the music, a pop-type production, and hit-single mentality with a straightforward, distinctively Christian message in the lyric. In short, she makes Christianity a totally positive experience, a joy to hear and sing. The second song is "Hosanna," which tells the story of the entrance of Jesus into Jerusalem on Palm Sunday.

"Unshakeable Kingdom," a big church ballad, delivers the message that the Kingdom of God is within you. Somehow Christians generally believe that the Kingdom of God is something to be strived for, something distant and remotely attainable—a bright, shining reward. The biblical admonition from Jesus that "the Kingdom of God is within you" has come too close to the modern philosophies of Zen Buddhism and Transcendental Meditation to allow American Christians to feel comfortable about it, but this song, written by Bill and Gloria Gaither, manages to hold a traditional view, while presenting a new insight that falls perfectly in line with mainstream Christianity.

Another ballad, "Shepherd of My Heart," follows. The song is unique because, although it is a "You" song, the "You" is unmistakable. Discussing the earlier "You" songs, Sandi said, "We kind of thought for a while that to get the attention of secular radio we had to compromise our lyrics. It just didn't work. Now everyone's serious about telling exactly what they feel and believe. The music's gotten better, and there is no compromise at all in the potentially life-changing words. And you know what? *Now* we're getting airplay. You've got to do what you do best—so now we're accomplishing what we set out to do in the beginning."

"Love in Any Language" is not a gospel song per se, but it probably has the strongest message on the album. Here, the faith is universal, expressed by love. "Love in Any Language" has strength and a totally captivating chorus and it ends Side One with a positive message of hope and reconciliation.

Side Two begins with another long intro and dramatic buildup before launching into "King of Glory," another up-tempo song. "Face to Faith" follows with some Bible stories with a moral, wrapped in vocal novelties that sound somewhat like Manhattan Transfer. Like "Pour on the Power" from her *Songs from the Heart* LP, this is a jazzy, upbeat, up-tempo number that adds a bit of spice and variety to the album and delivers the distinct message that Christianity can be fun.

"Morning Like This" is a Resurrection song that links biblical Christianity with contemporary life. Sandi loves the Resurrection songs and here she has one that is powerful with a new twist to the old story. Too, she makes the age-old faith fresh with this new perspective—a triumph for her, as she weaves this complex idea into a manageable concept.

"In the Name of the Lord," a song Sandi shares writing credit on (she wrote the music and some of the lyrics), deals with the divinity of Christ. It is a song of hope and encouragement—the theme of this album—as she presents a positive answer to life's negative questions.

The album closes with "There Is a Savior," a ballad that serves as a simple statement of faith. Since it closes the album, it is obvious that Sandi wants to leave her listeners with a very simple, obvious message. It also presents to the world-at-large the essence of Sandi's life and message in one song—here is the reason she sings, here is the reason you should agree with her and accept her faith as your own.

The album cover for *Morning Like This* presents a warmth (browns and red with Sandi holding a coffee cup) with breathtaking beauty (the sun rising over the mountains). It was definitely *not* taken at Sandi's home in the flatlands of Indiana! The total package represents a maturing of Sandi's talents as an artist and this album will definitely stand as a landmark album for her. It is fitting that it came in 1986—the year that would prove to be the apex of Sandi's career, both artistically and economically.

Morning Like This, with Word's clout behind it, zoomed to the top of the charts and, along with her *Hymns* album, dominated the charts throughout the year. The songs "Morning Like This" and "Let There Be Praise" were all over the airwaves as 1986 turned into the year of Sandi Patti in gospel music. When the dust had settled, five albums from Sandi—*Morning Like This, Hymns Just for You, Songs from the Heart, Live . . . More Than Wonderful,* and the re-released version of *Sandi's Songs*—had all been on the charts.

Sandi also appeared on another album this year, singing a duet with George Beverly Shea on his *George Beverly Shea and Friends* album on Word. Liner notes were written by Shea's longtime friend and partner, Billy Graham. Sandi has also sung on some of Graham's crusades, traveling to England with the evangelist in the summer of 1984 with her newborn daughter to sing for the audiences there.

First Call, who began touring at Sandi's instigation, released their *Undivided* album to rave reviews and the album soon had outstanding sales for a debut release. Their appearances on Sandi's Let There Be Praise tour catapulted them into the top ranks of contemporary Christian music. Indeed, in 1986 it seems as if everything Sandi Patti touched turned to gold.

Meanwhile, back in Indianapolis at the hospital, Sandi's brother Craig, who had been in a coma, was showing signs of a good recovery, with therapy administered several days a week and a stringent exercise program to get him back on his feet.

A true story Sandi told audiences about Craig's recovery that year involves her daughter Anna. It seems Sandi woke up one morning and heard Anna saying, "Hooray, Uncle Craig! Hooray, Uncle Craig! Thank you, Jesus!" and it was that very evening that Craig awoke from his coma. Sandi's dad asked his granddaughter later if she knew Uncle Craig was going to get better and she replied, matter-of-factly, "Uh-huh."

Sandi Patti turned thirty in 1986 and for this momentous occasion on July 12, she threw a party for her friends. "I did it because on your birthday you tend to think about why you are the way you are and about the people who have meant the most to you," she said. "I invited some of the ladies who have meant the absolute most to me in my life. We had a lunch, and I went around the room and introduced each person by telling the reason why she meant so much to me. We laughed and cried and had a wonderful time."

There was also another big reason to celebrate at this time—a few days before, something happened for Sandi Patti that would make her a household name.

37

It was a long weekend of feeling proud as Americans honored the icon of democracy—the Statue of Liberty—on her one hundredth anniversary. The Fourth of July weekend was a mixture of patriotism and profiteering, seen live and in color on the ABC network. Over six million people were on the island of Manhattan for this event and about twenty thousand boats were in New York Harbor, while the rest of the country sat home and watched.

The birthday bash featured a huge variety show, a twenty-tier stage with waterfalls, a cast that totaled twelve thousand, including a 476-member All-American Marching Band assembled from ninety-two colleges and universities, two hundred Elvis impersonators, Kenny Rogers, Willie Nelson, Elizabeth Taylor, Gregory Peck, the Temptations, the Four Tops, Frankie Avalon, Waylon Jennings, Billy Preston, Patti LaBelle, Shirley MacLaine, Gene Kelly, Liza Minnelli, the Pointer Sisters, Charlton Heston, Fabian, and Frank Sinatra.

One irony is that this was not really the statue's birthday—that wasn't until October 28, when a much more modest rededication was held—but that did not stop the flush of patriotic pride for the renovated statue. As President Reagan succinctly put it on Friday, July 4, when he pushed the button that lit the statue, "We are the keepers of the flame of liberty; we hold it high tonight for all the world to see."

But perhaps the greatest irony of all is that the biggest star to emerge from this mammoth celebration wasn't one of those who performed during the event or even someone who was at the celebration. She was a young lady just short of her thirtieth birthday who was at home in Anderson, Indiana, and did not even know she would be part of this celebration until her young daughter recognized her voice coming from the television set.

Sandi's spring tour had finished in Indianapolis in June. On the Fourth of July weekend, she was at home with her husband and daughter when ABC news anchor Peter Jennings, introducing the final segment said, "Over this weekend you've heard a lot of people sing who are famous, people who you see and hear almost every day. Somebody heard a woman sing 'The Star-Spangled Banner' not too long ago. She comes from Anderson, Indiana, and we thought you would like to hear it too. Her name is Sandi Patti." With that, Sandi's rendition of "The Star-Spangled Banner" began playing.

Neither Sandi nor John caught the introduction given by Peter Jennings, but when the song began, two-year-old Anna shouted, "Is that you singing, Mommy?" John and Sandi rushed to the television set and watched the film clip recapping the weekend's events—from the President's speech, the parade of tall clipper ships, new Americans taking the oath of citizenship, and performances of some of the top names in show business to the giant fireworks display in the sky above the Statue of Liberty while Sandi's rendition of the National Anthem played. When it finished, Peter Jennings closed, saying, "There isn't anything left to say."

Actually, there was a lot left to say, like: "Who is this Sandi Patti? And where did *she* come from?" That was the question many Americans watching the program were asking and more than a thousand phone calls came into the ABC switchboard. Perhaps it is a chilling recognition of the place of gospel music in this country that most Americans had never heard of Sandi Patti until this event —yet she had the top-selling gospel album in the country at the time, had a gold album hanging on her wall, was regularly filling concert halls, had won Grammy and Dove awards, and was generally acknowledged to be one of the two Gospel Superstars. (The other is Amy Grant.) But there are pockets of popularity and America is a nation of subcultures, so fame with one audience does not assure broad mass-appeal *fame* all across this country.

Earlier in 1986, Word Records had released an album entitled *They Come to America* that featured patriotic songs from Glen Campbell, Marie Osmond, Willie Nelson, Kate Smith, Leonard Bernstein, and Johnny Cash, in addition to Sandi's version of "The Star-Spangled Banner." The album was designated the official album for the statue's centennial and proceeds from the sale of the album were earmarked for the restoration fund. The album had been the brainstorm of Dan Johnson, a Word executive who wanted to tie his company in with the Statue of Liberty promotions and fund-raising in some way.

Word had sent a cassette of Sandi singing "The Star-Spangled Banner" to ABC, hoping the network would use it during the festivities. Roger Goodman, director of production and design for ABC, listened to the cassette on Friday and realized it would be a perfect closing for the celebration. He played the song for executive producer Roone Arledge the next day and the decision was made to use it. Since it was a holiday weekend, ABC was not able to notify Sandi in advance—thus the surprise when she heard it on television.

ABC decided to feature Sandi on "ABC World News Tonight" after the overwhelming response and flew a TV crew to Anderson to interview Sandi in her home. The segment aired at the conclusion of Monday evening's national news.

In the interview, Sandi told Angel Hawthorne, an ABC producer from Chicago, "It was the strangest feeling to be watching the liberty celebration at home with my family, and suddenly hearing myself singing on national television. I had no idea that was going to happen. I was shocked, but pleasantly shocked."

After this exposure, she received a call from those in charge of booking talent on "The Tonight Show," who arranged for her appearance with Johnny Carson. She was only supposed to sing "Pour on the Power" and "Love in Any Language" with the NBC orchestra and First Call. But just before she went on the air, one of the staffers told her that when she finished, to just put the microphone down and go over and have a seat with Johnny.

After the musical numbers, Sandi walked over and joined Carson, who broke for a commercial after the applause had subsided. When they returned, Sandi informed Carson that accepting the invitation to be on his show had caused her to turn down Vice President George Bush, who had invited her to meet with him in Washington. Carson looked at the camera and said, "Sorry, George," before continuing, with a smirk, "George has a lot of open dates."

On the next commercial break, Carson uttered a word he could not use on television, then became slightly embarrassed because he had cursed in front of a gospel singer. When the program returned to the air, Carson publicly apologized to Sandi, then asked her if she ever used profanity. Sandi replied, laughing, "Well, actually, no, I don't." Then Carson asked her what she would do if she accidentally hit her thumb "real hard" with a hammer. Sandi replied calmly that she would "probably call my husband's name for help."

There was a long pause while Carson tried to think of a response. Finally comedian Jay Leno, who had also performed on the show, said, "Somebody give me a hammer," as he and Carson both grabbed Sandi's thumb.

When the laughter subsided, Carson said to Sandi, "You have a great deal of control. It's nice to have those kinds of principles." As the program came to a close, he invited Sandi back for another appearance.

Sandi had a lot of butterflies before the Carson appearance, but prayed, "Lord, I feel this door has been opened by You, so I am going in Your name and I am going to trust that You're taking care of all the details." Sandi relates that everything fell into place. "When the Lord is in control of something, He doesn't miss a thing," she said. "People were praying all day that we would feel calm and that there would be an in-control feeling. That's exactly how I would describe that day. Sure, I was nervous. I remember thinking, 'This is not the time to forget the words!' " Telling the story of how she came to be interviewed by Carson, she notes, "It was a little bit off-the-cuff. But I'm glad I didn't know ahead of time."

Sandi performed at the Kennedy Center in Washington, D.C., when Word Music debuted their hymnal *The Hymnal for Worship and Celebration* during "An Evening of Worship and Celebration" at the thirty-seventh meeting of the Christian Booksellers' Association Convention. The capacity crowd of three thousand listened as a 50-piece orchestra under the direction of Robert Walters and a 200-voice choir directed by C. Harry Causey.

In August Sandi went to the Christian Artists Seminar for Europe, held in De Bron, Holland. There, under the thatched roof of the concert hall, she performed "Love in Any Language" and received a tremendous response. From here she went on to Germany, where she performed before some American military personnel.

At her first concert, in Kaiserslautern, about two thousand people showed up and in Erlangen the crowd was about one thousand. The concerts were sponsored by Youth with a Mission (YWAM) and organized by Eddie Huff, who had only three weeks to prepare for the events. The highlight of each evening was when the entire audience stood as Sandi began "The Star-Spangled Banner." In a note she sent to the YWAM staffers at the end of August after she returned, she said, "Singing for the military personnel was one of the most fulfilling things I have done in a long time . . . I really want to come back sometime."

For the European trip, she and John had left Anna at home. Sandi said, "I didn't realize how much I missed her until I heard her squeal at the airport."

The Let There Be Praise tour resumed the week of September 8 with thirty-five dates set between then and mid-December. In addition to the concerts, Sandi also performed on several major network television shows.

In December she performed before President and Mrs. Reagan in the NBC Special "Christmas from Washington." That made her the second person in the Patty clan to perform before a President of the United States. Interestingly, both Presidents—Reagan and Eisenhower (who was part of the audience when Sandi's father Ron performed with Fred Waring at the White House in 1957)—were both Republicans.

It was an evening filled with Sandi Patti's music—in addition to her solo of "Bethlehem Morning," five other songs she had recorded were used as the basis for the program's music. Sandi also sang (with the other guests) "Let There Be Praise," "King of Glory," "Worship the King," "O Holy Night," and a variation of Sandi's "Celebrate the Gift" medley.

On the closing number, as the entire cast took the stage, Sandi stood shoulder to shoulder with President Reagan while singing "Hark! The Herald Angels Sing." The next morning Sandi and John visited with George Bush in his White House office. Following the meeting, they were given a private tour of the White House.

Sandi sang "Merry Christmas with Love" from *The Gift Goes On* and a special medley of "Go Tell It on the Mountain" and "Amen" during her second Carson show appearance in December.

But the TV appearance with the largest potential viewing audience was on Christmas Eve. Titled "A Worldwide Christmas Celebration," the event was simulcast live from New York, London, Bethlehem, Sydney, Vienna, and other locations. Hosted by Raymond Burr, other luminaries included Prince Charles, Billy Graham, Placido Domingo, Cliff Richard, and the Vienna Boys Choir. On this show, Sandi performed "O Holy Night," "Bethlehem Morning," and "Love in Any Language."

The year 1986 was one of mixed blessings for Sandi Patti, a year of great triumphs and great sorrows. In October she began to announce during her concerts that she and John were expecting their second child in the spring. But ten and a half weeks into the pregnancy—just before Thanksgiving—she had a miscarriage. It was a crushing blow and Sandi wrote in her newsletter, "What hurt we felt, what a loss, what a very sad time . . . [but] through the valley we continued to *trust* in our Great Shepherd. Even when we didn't understand, we continued to *trust* . . . Even when the hurt was so great that it seemed impossible to go on, we continued to *trust.*"

Sandi spent Christmas at her home in Anderson with her family. Craig was recovering nicely and Anna got plenty of new toys, although her unborn child still had a place in Sandi's heart and mind. It was a year she would never forget—the peak of her career thus far.

Sandi thought of the incredible blessings she had received from doing the National Anthem. David T. Clydesdale's dramatic, soaring arrangement and the second verse composed by Claire Cloninger were good, logical reasons why the song was so well received. Yet, there was more to it than that—more than Sandi's tremendous God-given talent for singing. Somehow she could not help but feel that God had given her a special annointing with that song and she would be expected to carry that torch for the rest of her life.

It was an awesome feeling and Sandi must have felt some pride mixed with trepidation, some reassuring warmth in the midst of the cold December air as the snow fell in Anderson a few days after Christmas, covering the ground outside the cozy warmth in her home.

38

The rewards for 1986 came in the form of the awards of 1987. The first were the Grammys and Sandi carried home two—one for Gospel Vocal, Female, for her album, *Morning Like This* (ending Amy Grant's reign there) and the other one shared with Deniece Williams for their duet "They Say."

Deniece Williams, a former backup singer for Stevie Wonder, is best known for her pop hits "Let's Hear It for the Boy," which captured the ears of pop radio listeners in 1984, and her duet with Johnny Mathis, "Too Much, Too Little, Too Late," from 1978. In 1986 she released her first gospel album on Sparrow, *I Surrender All.* This album contains the single "They Say" and the duet features Sandi Patti in rare form.

"They Say" is an R&B ballad-type number, full of the high energy of black pop—with the lyrical message that "they" (the unbelievers) can't divert the singer from the truth. Sandi proves she has the vocal versatility to pull this off without sounding hokey or honkie and soulless—in fact, some of her fans smiled as they wondered how she could cook so well with "Niecey." Too, this duet underscores Sandi's continuing quest to help improve race relations with her music. Her three most popular duets have been with blacks—two with Larnelle Harris and one with Deniece Williams—and a black couple is pictured prominently on the back of her *Hymns Just for You* album. This duet also underscores the value of tying your star to others—three of Sandi's four Grammys have been shared, two with Larnelle and one with Deniece.

Sandi also performed "Let There Be Praise" during the Grammy telecast. It must have been quite a thrill to be singing while one of her heroes, Barbra Streisand, sat in the audience, watching. (Streisand won a Grammy for her *Broadway* album.)

The hot 1986 year for Sandi was further reflected in the February 1987 charts. Here, Sandi had four of the top ten—*Hymns Just for You* at number one, *Songs from the Heart* at number three, *Live . . . More Than Wonderful* at number four, and *Morning Like This* at number ten. "In the Name of the Lord" was number seven on the adult contemporary song chart and number two on the inspirational chart.

Amy Grant held down three positions in the top ten album charts. She and Sandi controlled 70 percent of the top ten albums as 1987 got under way. This reflected the dominant trend of the day—the big artists were getting bigger, while everybody else was trying to survive.

Sandi's next stop to pick up awards was at the eighteenth annual Dove Awards. That evening, it was difficult to determine whether the Gospel Music Association was putting on an awards show or a Sandi Patti special—she was connected to nine winners that night in some form or fashion.

The show had some bright spots—chief among them being a national sponsor for the first time. Chick-fil-A, an Atlanta-based firm that sells chicken in shopping malls, had come to Nashville on February 2 to make the big announcement. Sandi Patti, Bill Gaither, Amy Grant, and DeGarmo and Key all stood in front of reporters to say how wonderful Chick-fil-A is and how wonderful Gospel Music Week would be. The Chick-fil-A folks had been sponsoring Bill Gaither's concerts for several years and had begun sponsoring Sandi's concerts during the fall 1986 tour. This meant that Chick-fil-A paid these artists some money and in return got to show their banner and logo on ads, promotional materials, and during the concert. Sometimes it was arranged for the artist to stop by the local

Chick-fil-A mall location and sign albums or say howdy to folks coming by.

During the Dove show, Sandi picked up three awards for herself, including her fourth Artist of the Year honor, her sixth consecutive Female Vocalist Dove, and Inspirational Album of the Year for *Morning Like This.* In her acceptance comments, Sandi said that the most influential influences in her life were her parents, that "music is nothing without the message," and "it's so wonderful to have the support of the industry."

Backstage Sandi discussed her career. "I feel a continuing mission to challenge people to a deeper walk with the Lord." About her awards, she said, "Sometimes I check myself and ask, 'What is my motive?' And I can honestly say it is not awards but to do what I feel the Lord would have me do, encouraging other people." About her records, she said, "It's hard to know about a final product, what people will respond to. I don't try to please every single person, but I try to do what the Lord wants."

At another time she said, "My very strong Christian lyrics are appropriate for who I am singing for, but I think that I would have to soften them to get any kind of secular radio airplay. That just isn't something that I'm willing to do. I understand that my music probably wouldn't be accepted by a lot of people and that's fine. I'm very comfortable with what I'm doing."

Sandi and her producer, Greg Nelson, were standing backstage when it was announced that Dick and Melody Tunney had won the Songwriter of the Year honor. Both Sandi and Greg ran out of the room to the backstage area where Dick and Melody were coming after receiving their award. A scream was heard and there were a lot of hugs. Sandi told Melody, "Save this envelope [which had held the winners' names] and frame it!"

In addition to the Songwriter of the Year award, Dick and Melody Tunney also won the Dove for Song of the Year with their song "I've Just Seen Jesus" (written with Paul Smith), while First Call won two Doves—Group of the Year and the Horizon award for the best new act. (That made Melody Tunney the top Dove winner in 1987 with four of the heavy birds.)

After the show was over, Sandi said, "I feel like a quarterback who gets a lot of credit and attention but knows that without a great team it wouldn't be possible," before thanking her husband John, the Helvering Agency, and the concert promoters "for all they do." She added that, for the future, "I'll keep on doing what I've been doing." Previously she had said, "The Grammy and Dove awards mean something very important to me . . . [but] they haven't changed my goals or perspective. I would be doing what I'm doing whether or not there were Doves or Grammys."

But Dick Tunney summed up best what it is like to receive a major award when he said, at the end of the Doves, "I'm pretty overwhelmed."

The Dove Awards had capped off a busy week for Sandi, full of activities, honors, and awards. She had arrived in town Sunday night with a whole contingent of staffers and checked into the Hermitage Hotel. On Monday morning, at the annual Gospel Music Association's meeting, she was given a special award for her contributions and achievements in gospel music. Amy Grant also received this award from the GMA. These awards pointed to a conclusion many in gospel music had come to realize—gospel music in 1987 was, in many ways, a two-headed creature, one head belonging to Sandi Patti and the other to Amy Grant. But though these two heads are looking in two different directions, they are connected to the same body.

Sandi hosted a "Koffee Klatch" during GMA Week that featured coffee, doughnuts, and juice for registrants. Sandi was a gracious hostess, smiling and greeting people at eight in the morning, shaking hands, chatting, and having her picture taken. At the BMI luncheon that day, Sandi received her first songwriting award (for "In the Name of the Lord," which had been nominated for a Dove in the Song of the Year category). She and John received a publisher's award for their publishing company, Sandi's Songs, for "In the Name of the Lord." Greg Nelson, Sandi's producer, also received some awards and Joe Moscheo, BMI executive and host for the event, pointed out that Nelson had written or produced nine of the ten songs nominated for a Dove in the Song of the Year category.

Sandi exerted a powerful influence on the Song of the Year nominees. She was responsible for popularizing four of the ten nominees—"In the Name of the Lord," "Morning Like This," "Let There Be Praise," and "Love in Any Language"—and had performed a duet with Larnelle Harris on a fifth song, "I've Just Seen Jesus."

Also during the BMI luncheon, Sandi was presented with three gold albums from two different companies. First, Benson executives presented Sandi with gold albums for *Songs from the Heart* and *Hymns Just for You.* One executive gave a short speech, saying how much he admired Sandi, and then made a somewhat subtle pitch for her to return to the label, saying, "We had a few problems in the past that I hope can be resolved." Word executive Dan Johnson followed that with a gracious reference to the Benson folks and Sandi's talents and he presented Sandi with a gold album for her first Word release, *Morning Like This.*

Sandi showed her professionalism and cool in the spotlight by thanking both companies and saying, "When it's all said and done, we're not just a bunch of companies and a bunch of different people, we're all people trying to get across the same message—that Jesus Christ is the Lord."

More big news came when it was officially announced that Sandi would be changing booking agencies. Her longtime association with Spring House would end after concerts set for later in 1987. She would then be represented by the large secular firm of William Morris. Steve Brallier, the agent who handles her concerts, would also leave Spring House and move to William Morris, so the team would stay intact. Brallier was formerly with the public relations department at Anderson College before being hired by Bill Gaither to handle bookings and concert promotions at Spring House.

After the Doves, Sandi gathered up her awards and headed

back to Anderson in the dark of the night. In less than twenty-four hours, she would be on the stage at Anderson High School, performing a concert for her hometown family and friends—one of four concerts remaining on the Let There Be Praise tour. As the miles fell away and she drifted off to sleep, Sandi could think of no better place she would like to be heading toward than Anderson, Indiana, and home sweet home. She also realized that a much greater award than any she had received during the GMA Week was growing within her—she and John were expecting a baby later in the year. She had not announced it, though. After the miscarriage, she wanted to wait and be *sure* everything would be all right. She closed her eyes, smiled, and put her hand across her stomach—it seemed as if it would be.

39

The honeymoon for Christianity and the conservative movement that began in early 1977 with the inauguration of Jimmy Carter—the first "born-again" President—ended in the spring of 1987. The PTL and Iran-Contra scandals left the righteous right exposed in ways that severely damaged the public trust and created a cynicism toward the high and mighty in this movement.

The question is always asked: "What skeletons are in the closet?" The assumption is that there are *always* skeletons in the closet. Until the spring of 1987, the Christian culture had been able to say there were none and be believable, although there had long been a distrust from the secular press toward the televangelists because of the large amount of money coming into their coffers. But after the spring scandals, the Christian culture itself had to come to grips with what it always tried to deny: There are skeletons in the closet and sometimes they are found.

The PTL Club (for "Praise the Lord" or "People That Love") was first rocked by the news that Tammy Faye Bakker would be entering the Betty Ford Center for Drug Rehabilitation in California because of her abuse of over-the-counter drugs during the preceding seventeen years. Then the organization—as well as the rest of the country—was shocked to learn that host Jim Bakker had had a sexual affair with a church secretary named Jessica Hahn in 1980. More scandalous news followed, and other sexual revelations were hinted at. When Bakker was defrocked by his Assembly of God peers, Jerry Falwell, former head of the Moral Majority, took over the network and engaged in a public tugging match with the Bakkers for control of the remaining faithful. Along the way it was discovered there were vast financial improprieties, including over $90 million missing, and the lavish lifestyle of the Bakkers was disclosed.

Out in Tulsa, Oklahoma, evangelist Oral Roberts announced that God was holding him ransom for $8 million and if the faithful flock did not come through soon he would be "called home." Just in the nick of time, a dog track owner—who admitted he didn't go to church—gave Oral the needed money. Oral smiled and had his picture taken accepting the money with the gentleman, although he had previously campaigned against racing because it is sinful. Later, in the summer, Oral made claims of raising the dead while trying to raise some more support for his 400-acre complex (particularly his medical facility), then began to hedge as some demanded proof.

In Washington, President Reagan faced his toughest battle as a parade of witnesses sat in front of a congressional committee and told of arms deals to the Iranians with resulting profits that either disappeared, went into the pockets of arms dealers, or went to the Nicaraguan Contras. Earlier, Reagan had been accused of having a "sleaze factor" in his government because over 100 members of his administration had been indicted, investigated, or shown to have problems with ethics as well as the law of the land. On Wall Street, greed was running amuck as the stock market was acting like a yo-yo. Investigators were trying to rein in avarice as insider trading scandals were sending more rich and powerful executives to prison. Through it all, public trust in the President, Wall Street, and Christianity was ebbing.

The presidential race for the 1988 election claimed its first victim in the spring of 1987 when Gary Hart droppped out after some revelations about his alleged sexual escapades came to light. On the Republican side, Pat Robertson, founder of "The 700

Club," watched as his support eroded in the wake of the scandals involving American Christianity.

Yes, the honeymoon had ended for the Christian revival that begat the Christian culture for the last ten years. The American public became increasingly disgusted and cynical about the most visible figures in this movement—the televangelists. When the news stopped flowing, it was obvious that, as evangelist Jimmy Swaggart observed, "The Gospel of Jesus Christ has sunk to an all-time low."

On the radio, "Would Jesus Wear a Rolex on His Television Show?" was becoming a popular song. Over in Charlotte, North Carolina, at the PTL complex, this organization was appealing to Christian musicians to help restore some order, integrity, and credibility. Jerry Falwell had enlisted the support of Bill Gaither in booking artists on the show—but it was like being put on the *Titanic*'s entertainment committee *after* it had hit the iceberg.

The seeds for this fall from grace had been planted long before. Many leaders in the Christian culture (including a number of artists and musicians) have long represented a home-grown radicalism that carries with it a deep-seated disrespect for institutions and rules: They believed in what they were doing and that they received their authority from God. In general, they "thought" very little but "felt" a great deal because, theologically, the "born-again" movement put emphasis on direct experience rather than knowledge or ritual practice. This Christianity, by its very nature, is anti-intellectual, unhistoric, and focuses its attention on the quality of will rather than the record of past deeds—good or bad. Their guiding philosophy is the "justification by faith," which became, in essence, a license for the believer to do whatever he felt like doing. Thus, the popular bumper sticker CHRISTIANS AREN'T PERFECT, JUST FORGIVEN signifies both a great truth and a great mockery in this movement.

For those outside the Christian culture, a massive cynicism colored their view of Christianity. However, such observations from those looking in are the norm. Outsiders are quick to point out the hypocrisy of professional Christians; they're easy prey because a certain amount of hypocrisy is inherent in Christianity. This comes from man trying to serve God—and be like Jesus—while at the same time having the basic nature of a human being. Thus, there is a constant push and pull between heavenly desires and earthly temptations and foibles among believers. Their deep conviction that they have the authority of God as a stamp of approval often leads to a spiritual arrogance that manifests itself in an "us versus them" society where all group members are entirely good while all outsiders are entirely bad, inferior, and untrustworthy. Furthermore, they may see all those who disagree with them as evil and immoral.

This practice of an individual aligning himself with God can be a great strength and appeal of Christianity, but when it becomes perverted and abused, it can be the great undoing of a Christian movement. Few would argue that the undoing of the Christian culture's heyday came about because of this arrogance and grandiose sense that normal rules and laws do not apply to oneself.

It became apparent that the Christian culture was a house divided, with one group trying to live the good life—Christian style—surrounded by Christian materialism (books, records, and so on) in a totally Christian environment, while another group was trying to haul America back to some mythical era of God-fearing virtue. Then there was a third group, trying simply to live by the light, taking one day at a time in a simple and earnest attempt to put the Gospel into daily practice.

As money became the measure of achievement and success, those who were not making it hand over fist began to feel like suckers and it was hard to resist jumping into this race. Many self-professed Christians could not resist and plunged right in. What was lost along the way was a sense of public responsibility.

In America fame is secular sainthood. Perhaps it is not surprising—given the Christian culture's demand for celebrities and the desire of many individual Christians to be celebrities—that Christians would fall prey to this temptation. Still, it was disconcerting to see the rewards received by some of those who fell so far from grace.

In the gospel music world, all of the major record labels found themselves in trouble in 1987. Zondervan, owner of the Benson labels, had to fight off a hostile takeover that left it financially drained. Word, which had been purchased by a giant conglomerate, was told to come up with more profits. Sparrow was also in financial straits and there were a number of reports in the industry that gospel artists were missing royalty payments, while a number of former record company executives found themselves in the unemployment lines.

By the end of 1987, it was no longer fashionable to be a Christian, no longer a badge of honor to broadcast that you were "born again." That does not mean that Christianity itself is coming to an end—the faith has weathered much more difficult storms than this—nor does it mean that gospel music will no longer be heard or sung. But the optimism that gospel can be "the next big thing" or even that there is a huge potential market just waiting for the right combination of things and people is gone.

The financial backbone of Christian music has never been in records; it is in publishing. The tragedy of the contemporary Christian music movement is that those in this movement thought it *would* be in records as the Christian culture unfolded. Because they used the pop music culture as an inspiration and ideal, the Christian music community sought to emulate the pop world with its stars, big concert tours, and platinum albums. But the success of contemporary Christian artists never quite measured up.

The financial backbone of Christian music lies in print music—sheet music, songbooks, folios, and song collections. This print music is purchased by choirs and churches so the songs can be sung in the sanctuary. It wasn't until Sandi Patti—and the rediscovery of the inspirational market—that the Christian music industry remembered this. Sandi Patti's success stems directly from the fact that she sings songs that can be sold as print music to choirs in churches. These songs can be sung during regular church services or on special programs because they fit in a church setting. And the church remains the cornerstone of Christianity. In spite of the intents and attempts of contemporary Christian musicians to compete for pop music's audience, the church world has always been the foundation for gospel music. This has been proven in the past and will be proven again in the future.

The big artists will remain big artists, but it will be increasingly difficult for new unknown acts to make their mark. For Sandi Patti, who came to fame before this all hit, it will not mean the loss of a career. But it may be more difficult to pack large concert halls and gold records may be a little more scarce. Still, she has developed a solid organization and has worked hard to be in a position where trends and fads will not affect her as greatly as they will other artists.

In May 1987 Sandi Patti sang in Washington at an after-dinner concert with Steve Green for the National Day of Prayer Banquet. Among the guest speakers was Ronald Reagan. And she sang the National Anthem later that month during the Memorial Day weekend for the start of the Indianapolis 500, as well as for the Pan-American Games in the summer. She also sang at the Constitution celebration in Philadelphia and during the Pope's visit to this country in September.

Sandi's future is becoming clear and obvious. When America needs a dose of patriotism or religion in song, Sandi Patti will be called upon. And Sandi will be there at all the big events. In some way it is an enviable position, in other ways it is a drawback. It is difficult to be a contemporary act in the music world and be an "institution" at the same time. Still, one suspects that twenty or thirty years down the line, when someone must sing the National Anthem at a major event, or sing a gospel song for the nation, it will be Sandi Patti's name that comes up first. And in between these big events, Sandi will continue to record gospel albums and sing for the traditional church audience, who will remain Christians whether it is in style or not.

40

The concert crowd ambles back to their seats, milling around in small groups. A lot of churches have brought youth groups tonight, and they are clearly excited, giggling among themselves. Some are holding their Sandi Patti sweatshirts, others are wearing them. Some little children with T-shirts are beginning to look a bit tired.

The merchandising at a concert generally provides the profit for a road tour. The markups are large—the sweatshirts generally cost around $5.00 to $8.00 and are sold for $20.00. Since this is the end of the tour and they are trying to get rid of the merchandise, the prices are slashed—short-sleeved T-shirts are a going for $4.00 for kids, $5.00 for adults. The recorded product has a smaller markup and is not as profitable; albums at Sandi's concerts go for $9.00. It must be said for Sandi that, unlike many other artists, she has generally avoided the urge to be greedy and has not gouged the fans who purchase her merchandise.

The concert ticket prices are also pretty reasonable at Sandi's concerts, especially considering the cost of concerts in general. On this evening, the tickets are priced at $10.50 and $9.50, with $8.50 the price for the nosebleed sections. She will gross about $75,000 this evening. On thirteen dates during the spring 1987 tour, Sandi played before 65,413 people, averaging 5,032 per night. Only two concerts were sellouts and two others saw only half the hall filled. It's rough on the concert trail and everybody in gospel music is taking a beating, looking for audiences. The good news is that Sandi is not taking quite as bad a beating as a lot of other acts. Even with concert attendance for Christian concerts way down, she and Amy Grant and a few others still manage to do all right. From these thirteen dates, Sandi grossed about $650,000 from ticket sales.

Sandi makes the highest net income of anyone in gospel music. The reason is that she does not carry a band—she performs to "tracks" or instrumental accompaniments to her songs. These are the same tracks heard on the albums, except Sandi's voice is not on them. These track accompaniments are available to her fans at the concert or through mail order, so anyone can stand in their living room or bedroom and be just like Sandi Patti, singing along to the same musical background. It is an appeal many find hard to resist.

These instrumental tracks assure Sandi that the same arrangement will be played each night—important to Sandi because she does not like surprises when she is performing. Also, the tracks "don't talk back," as she once observed. It saves the cost of musicians as well, which can average about $500 per concert for top musicians. Instead, she has one musician—Dick Tunney—who plays keyboards along with the tracks. The added effect of a live musician is considerable and allows her to sing with just the piano for a nice balance. Too, it gives another body onstage for some repartee, which is essential in a two-and-a-half-hour evening.

During the break, a number of people run into friends from their congregation and stop to chat. Just about everyone here at this concert tonight will be sitting in church on Sunday—many singing in the choir—and this underscores the point that the church remains the bedrock for gospel music. Since the Jesus Revolution, many young Christian artists fled from the church because they wanted to reach a different audience, because the church did not accept their music, or because they were simply uncomfortable there. No so with Sandi Patti; the church is her home.

The church has openly embraced Sandi, as evidenced by the number of Dove Awards she has received. She is their kind of person and their kind of singer. Amy Grant has received the most attention from the secular world for gospel music, but Sandi Patti is the artist most honored *within* the gospel world. Her concerts seem more like a worship service as she stands onstage, leading the worship, accepting that each member of the audience believes what she believes, accepts what she accepts. She does nothing to challenge their faith; she accepts and encourages it. And the church knows that Sandi is one of their own, an ordinary believer with an incredible God-given talent to sing better than any other soprano church soloist.

Sandi loves her audiences and has noted that sometimes she stands backstage about ten minutes before the concert begins, just watching them, soaking in the excitement and their love. She is careful not to develop a stage persona that is radically different from her offstage self and has commented that she desires to present an extension of who she is while onstage, using music to communicate. She's learned this from the Gaithers—to just be yourself onstage, treating the audience as if they are friends sitting in your living room, having coffee. It is this genuineness, this basic down-to-earth approach to life and show biz, that creates the "warmth" at a Sandi Patti concert.

Back at the soundboard, husband John has returned and Sandi is ready to sing again, secure knowing he's back there. Anyone who is around Sandi Patti for any length of time at all knows she is hopelessly devoted to her husband. Sandi says John "does so many things. He's a very unique man. People see that I'm pretty much at ease onstage, but they don't realize that I know that John is back there on the soundboard, and that on a certain word I know the tape is going to start and I don't have to worry if a guy is paying attention."

Sandi adds, "There has never been a time when there was a difficulty with me being in the forefront and John being in the background. John feels that what he is doing is what God has given him to do. Although people may not see him very much, John is just a part of everything I do and everything that I am. He's in control of everything." At another time, Sandi said, "There are many things about John that astound me. Sometimes I sit back and look at all he does and it amazes me. I think, 'My goodness, if I had known this, I would have grabbed him a lot sooner!' "

There is a certain appeal to the reluctant star, the person who has achieved stardom and claims he or she really wasn't after it. This is something Sandi has claimed, but it is basically true because it has been John who has been the driving force in her career. Sandi has admitted that it is John who always had the vision for what she is doing and this means that it has been his planning, foresight, and ambition that have propelled her forward. She has not fought against this, but neither has she had to fight against her own dreams of success and stardom to be where she is today. This gives her a clear conscience about her success, while other Christian artists often have a hard time reconciling themselves to ambition for stardom and having "the heart of a servant" at the same time.

But it is not always easy on Sandi—this life in the spotlight. "There are times when the traveling gets to be really hectic. And sometimes when we're getting ready for a trip I think, 'Oh, if I could just stay home for a couple more days.' But once I get to a concert and see the faces of so many people who are there to praise God, it just makes all of those other things seem trivial."

Sandi said in an interview once, "I know this is going to sound a little weird, but many times when I'm onstage I feel that I'm kind of a third party to the whole thing, just standing back and watching what's going on. I feel that the Lord is singing through me . . . through my voice or through my body. He's communicating, using what I have to offer Him with which to communicate. I can say with all honesty that I know I could not be doing what I'm doing without the Lord's leading."

During the concert program, there is always a segment when Sandi and the singers do a selection of hymns. Sandi begins by singing "Blessed Assurance." An instrumental version of "In the Garden" comes next and the audience sings the chorus. Melody Tunney then steps up and does "What a Friend We Have in Jesus," followed by Bonnie Keen doing "Great Is Thy Faithfulness" and

Marty McCall doing "Amazing Grace," with all the singers joining together at the end. It has become obvious that Sandi and the audience feel part of a family—each would say they are part of the family of God—and a "family feeling" pervades the hall as another member of the audience comes to the front of the stage and leaves some more roses for Sandi.

Now comes the part of the program where Sandi shares her "message." It begins on a humorous note as she tells about singing the National Anthem before the Chicago Bears and Los Angeles Rams playoff game in January 1986. She tells about the sound check at 9:30 A.M. before an empty stadium and on an empty field, then tells what it was like with a stadium full of screaming football fans and huge football players hulking about—running on the field as she is trying to get off. She compares that with her everyday life and says, "The Lord has called me to do something, prepared me, equipped me—but I panic. I can't see because of all the giants in the way. There are doubts, disappointments, heartaches, burdens, decisions, loss of a loved one, unconfessed sin, unforgiveness, broken relationships, memories held captive." Then Sandi admonishes the audience that they can "do all things through Christ. It is He who strengthens me. The giants don't go away, but they do become a little less important, a little less significant." It is a quiet kind of preaching and the message seems simple—take on life with confidence, give your fears to God, don't get buffaloed by "life." But it is a message hard to live and so many in the audience see their own life ruled by fear, themselves held back by obstacles and adversaries. Sandi prods them gently to have heart, have faith, and have courage.

After this talk, Sandi does "Shepherd of My Heart," then "In the Name of the Lord," and finally "We Shall Behold Him" in front of a blue backdrop that shows white clouds. She uses sign language in the chorus to illustrate the song and her voice fills the auditorium; listeners sit in their chairs and feel a chill up their spines. No wonder she has been dubbed "The Voice" in gospel music circles. Finally she finishes and the whole audience rises en masse and gives her a tremendous standing ovation as she strides offstage.

It's easy to tell when a performer has planned an encore—the house lights stay off. Sandi and First Call don't stay offstage too long before returning to do "How Majestic Is Your Name." She walks off again, but you don't leave an audience after a rousing up-tempo number—you've got 'em wanting more—so Sandi again returns, bringing back Dick Tunney, and closes with a ballad. When this quiet number is finished, Sandi walks offstage, toward the backdrop that looks like a night sky filled with twinkling stars.

Epilogue

Sandi stands in the darkened hotel room by the window and looks out at the moonlit landscape. If there is a perfect moment for Sandi, it would be walking by the sea in the moonlight—hearing the waves, smelling the salty sea, feeling the breeze blowing from the water lit by the round full moon.

John and Anna are both asleep. Sandi looks at her sleeping child and is filled with an overwhelming, overpowering love. Anna is the center of her universe, the object of her most intense care.

She watches her daughter sleep and knows why she always overpacks—so Anna will always have a sweater when there's a chill, some play clothes when it is nice, something when it rains. (Didn't she once hear that whenever a mother gets cold, her child always has to put on a sweater?) She fusses over her family like a mother hen, a bundle of caring love for them. Does she nag too much? Yes, sometimes. Is she too possessive? Yes, at times it seems so. But that is how she shows her love, how she expresses herself best. It is how you are a mother.

Sandi goes over to the bed and tucks the covers up around little Anna. She remembers her mother doing little things for her and often wondered, as she grew up, if anyone could ever care for her as much as her mother. It is a fact—if you want to stay on Sandi's good side, don't ever criticize her mother! Or her, either. Sandi does not take criticism well, cannot look at it as objective. It always stings, it always hurts. Perhaps that is a reason why being in the spotlight is so difficult—all the criticism from strangers who don't even know her, don't understand her.

Still, she tries to accept all this. For every gain there is a loss, and the more success she gains, the more privacy she loses. Sandi wonders if there will ever be a true balance she will be comfortable with. Sometimes things just seem so out of control. She's not a person anymore—she's a whole business, a corporation.

Sandi worries about her weight. Is she putting on too many pounds? Does she need to diet more? Will audiences accept her? Sandi loves food, but wants to lose weight—and life on the road is a series of restaurants.

Tomorrow they will be going back to Anderson, back to her own home and her own bed. She can hardly wait. But first there is a concert and people to meet and hands to shake and smiles to give.

Now, however, is a time for prayer, for talking with God—for hearing God talk to her. She often reads her Bible at times like this. But tonight she feels a bit restless. And that's no way to feel when you've got to pack in the morning, do a concert, and then head home! She knows she needs to get some sleep.

Sandi stands at the window a moment longer before turning back to the bed. She crawls in and, putting her head on her pillow, closes her eyes. She feels the new life moving within her. Yes, the doctor said there will be two and they should be here by Christmas. She thinks about being a mother of three children—it will be a challenge! Tomorrow night she will be in her own bed again . . . but there are miles to go before she sleeps there. And in between, there are promises she must keep.

Awards

1982: Dove—Female Vocalist

Dove—Gospel Artist of the Year

also: Dove for Song of the Year for "We Shall Behold Him," which was popularized by Sandi

1983: Dove—Female Vocalist

Dove—Inspirational Album (for *Lift Up the Lord)*

Grammy nomination—Best Gospel Performance, Contemporary (for *Lift Up the Lord)*

1984: Dove—Female Vocalist

Dove—Gospel Artist of the Year

Dove—Inspirational Album (for *Live . . . More Than Wonderful)*

Dove—as coproducer of *Live . . . More Than Wonderful*

also: Dove for Song of the Year for "More Than Wonderful," which was popularized by Sandi

Grammy—Best Gospel Performance, Duo or Group (for "More than Wonderful" with Larnelle Harris)

Grammy nomination—Best Gospel Performance, Female (for *The Gift Goes On)*

1985: Dove—Female Vocalist

Dove—Gospel Artist of the Year

Dove—Inspirational Album (for : *Songs from the Heart)*

Dove—as coproducer of *Songs from the Heart*

also: Dove for Song of the Year for "Upon This Rock," which was popularized by Sandi

Grammy nomination—Best Gospel Performance, Female (for *Songs from the Heart)*

Gold Album—for *Live . . . More Than Wonderful*

1986: Dove—Female Vocalist

Grammy—Best Gospel Performance, Duo or Group (for "I've Just Seen Jesus" with Larnelle Harris)

Grammy nomination—Best Gospel Performance, Female (for *Hymns Just for You)*

also: Dove for Song of the Year for "Via Dolorosa," which was popularized by Sandi

Billboard's Inspirational Artist of the Year

Gold Album—for *Morning Like This*

Gold Album—for *Hymns Just for You*

1987: Dove—Female Vocalist

Dove—Gospel Artist of the Year

Dove—Inspirational Album (for *Morning Like This)*

Dove—as coproducer of *Morning Like This*

also: Dove for Song of the Year for "I've Just Seen

Jesus," which was popularized by Sandi and Larnelle Harris

Grammy—Best Gospel Performance, Female (for *Morning Like This)*

Grammy—Best Gospel Performance, Duo or Group (for "They Say" with Deniece Williams)

Discography

Major Solo Releases

Sandi's Song (1979)
Producer: Neal Joseph
Benson RO3724 (Originally released on Singspiration)

Side One:

"Jesus Is My Love Song to You"

"You're Such a Comfort to Me"

"When I Need Him"/"Precious Lord, Take My Hand"

"He'll Never Let You Down"

"I Could Never Have Imagined"

Side Two:

"You Never Gave Up on Me"

"The Day He Wore My Crown"

"It's All Right Now"

"The Devil Is a Liar"

"Sandi's Song (My Life Is a Song)"

Love Overflowing (1981)
Producer: Neal Joseph
Impact R3742

Side One:

"Down in My Heart"

"Keeper of the Well"

"Love Overflowing"

"So Far"

"When the Time Comes"

Side Two:

"The Home of the Lord"

"Somebody Believed"

"In His Hand"

"We Shall Behold Him"

"I Will Praise Him"

Lift Up the Lord (1982)
Producer: Greg Nelson
Impact R3799

Side One:

"Lift Up the Lord"

"How Majestic Is Your Name"

"They Could Not"

"Let Us Rejoice"

"Jesus, Lord to Me"

Side Two:

"I Will Lift You There"

"Let Him Hold Your Heart"

"Yes, God Is Real"

"Jesus You're Everything"

Reprise: "Jesus, Lord to Me"

Live . . . More Than Wonderful (1984)
Producers: Greg Nelson, David T. Clydesdale, Sandi Patti Helvering
Impact R3818

Side One:

"It's Your Song Lord"

"How Majestic Is Your Name"

"In His Love"

Medley: "Jesus Loves Me"

"Upon This Rock"

Side Two:

"Because of Who You Are"

"Yes, God Is Real"

"More Than Wonderful" (Duet with Larnelle Harris)

"When the Time Comes"

"We Shall Behold Him"

The Gift Goes On (1983)
Producer: Greg Nelson, Sandi Patti Helvering, and David T. Clydesdale
Impact RO3874

Side One:

"Worship the King"

"Worship the Gift" (Medley: "It Came Upon a Midnight Clear"/"Away in a Manger"/"What Child is This"/"O Little Town of Bethlehem")

"The Gift Goes On"

"Christmas Was Meant for Children"

"Jesu Bambino"/"O Holy Night"

Side Two:

Reprise: "Worship the King"

"Celebrate the Gift" (Medley: "Rejoice"/"For Unto Us a Child Is Born"/"Hark! The Herald Angels Sing"/"Joy to the World")

"I Wonder as I Wander"

"O Magnify the Lord"

"Bethlehem Morning"

"Merry Christmas with Love"/"Have Yourself a Merry Little Christmas"

Songs from the Heart (1984)
Producers: Greg Nelson and Sandi Patti Helvering
Impact RO3884

Side One:

"Give Him the Glory"

"Sing to the Lord"

"We Will See Him as He Is"

"Cradle Song"

"Wonderful Lord"

"Via Dolorosa"

Side Two:

"Shine Down"

"Pour on the Power"

"Glorious Morning"

"Purest Praise"

"The Stage Is Bare"

Hymns Just for You (1985)
Producers: Sandi Patti Helvering and Greg Nelson
Helvering Productions (Distributed by the Benson Company)
RO3910

Side One:

"It Is Well with my Soul"
Medley: "Fairest Lord Jesus"/"I'd Rather Have Jesus"
"How Great Thou Art"
Medley: "In the Garden"/"Just a Closer Walk"/"What a Friend We Have in Jesus"
"The Old Rugged Cross"

Side Two:

"The Lord's Prayer"
"Amazing Grace"
Medley: "To God Be the Glory"/"Holy, Holy, Holy"/"Blessed Assurance"/"Great Is Thy Faithfulness"
Medley: "A Mighty Fortress"/"Rock of Ages"/"Victory in Jesus"/"Because He Lives"
Medley: "Sweet Hour of Prayer"/"I Need Thee Every Hour"/"Just as I Am"/"Turn Your Eyes Upon Jesus"

Morning Like This (1986)
Producers: Greg Nelson and Sandi Patti Helvering
Word 7-01-900310-9

Side One:

"Let There Be Praise"
"Hosanna"
"Unshakeable Kingdom"
"Shepherd of My Heart"
"Love in Any Language"

Side Two:

"King of Glory"
"Face to Faith"
"Was It a Morning Like This"
"In the Name of the Lord"
"There Is a Savior"